HUMAN CONDITION SERIES: VOLUME I

Love, Demystified

Dr Jasmine, the family doctor

Love, God and electromagnetic energy are all the same thing
Romantic love is a rainbow, and you've got to taste all of its colours

Published in 2024 by Makesenseofyourworld Publishing Ltd

Text, original fiction and poetry © Dr Jasmine, 2024
Cover artwork © Dr Jasmine, 2024
All other paitings © Dr Jasmine, 2024
"Lone wolf" © HC, 2024
"Ismiidaamin" © Nashira Karasu, 2024

Figure 6: ID 24509367 © Alila07 | Dreamstime.com
Figure 8: Technology Vectors by Vecteezy

All rights reserved

This book or any portion thereof may not be reproduced or used in any manner whatsoever without the express written permission of the publishers except for the use of brief quotations in a book review. No portion of this book may be reproduced in any form without written permission from the publisher or author, except as permitted by copyright law.

This book contains works of fiction. Unless otherwise indicated, all the names, characters, places, events and incidents in this book are either the product of the author's imagination or used in a fictitious manner. Any resemblance to actual persons, living or dead, or actual events is purely coincidental.

ISBN 978-1-0686566-0-6

Typesetting and ebook production by Laura Kincaid
Ten Thousand | Editing + Book Design
www.tenthousand.co.uk

Contents

INTRODUCTION	1
CHAPTER 1: UNIVERSE MADE EASY	3
How does the universe work: an overview	3
Love: your connection with the universe	13
What is the purpose of your life?	17
What is the purpose of the universe?	22
How does the universe work: in detail	24
Love: metaphysical and human	26
Happiness: metaphysical and human	28
CHAPTER 2: THE ANATOMY OF LOVE	32
The role of romantic love	32
Fall in love and stay in love	35
One-night stand? No thank you!	37
The question of a soulmate	40
The power of romantic love	42
Will you be my muse?	46
The tragedy of romantic love	48
Love and marriage	52
Love is the drug	53
CHAPTER 3: THE COLOURS OF LOVE	57
Love is a rainbow	58
The colour red	59
The formula of passion	60

The shades of red	65
The colour orange	78
The prey and a hunter	79
The colour yellow	81
The colour green	84
The colour blue	89
The colour purple	91
Killing me softly	93
Unbearable	96
The colour black	99
The colour white	102
CHAPTER 4: IN LOVE WITH THE UNIVERSE	105
How you connect to the universe	105
Transcendence	105
Mind, body and heart	114
Eternal	116
How the universe connects to you	120
The role of a human	120
Hope, faith and love	122

Introduction

The world doesn't make sense, so why should I paint the pictures that do?

— Pablo Picasso

Dear Friend, there are different ways to describe love, life and the universe. I would like to share mine with you, and I hope that you will find this book helpful, or at least entertaining. Having had the privilege of witnessing many aspects of life of around a third of a million people in the course of my work as a family doctor, I feel that a human being/human society is a fair subject for my pen. Some of you might agree with my views, others not. I hope that I will not accidentally offend anyone; I am merely stating my opinion.

As the quote above states, it is often difficult to make sense of the world around us; this makes us feel out of control and uncomfortable.

Shall we try and solve the mystery of the universe together?

With love,

Dr Jasmine

CHAPTER I
Universe Made Easy

HOW DOES THE UNIVERSE WORK: AN OVERVIEW

People confuse models of reality with reality itself. Only when thought and emotion are combined can we understand reality.

– Bateson

All, everything that I understand, I understand only because I love.

– Leo Tolstoy

Dear Friend, do you find it easy to be happy, relaxed and contented, or do you struggle sometimes?

If it's the latter – many of us feel like that. Humans are trying to navigate the world armed with science and evidence, but somehow, it just does not work; maybe Tolstoy and Bateson are wise in suggesting a different angle.

Conventional science does NOT allow any emotion into its realm. Perhaps this is why human society is failing, and an individual human often feels himself a failure, too. Let us agree to be broad-minded in our approach to explaining the world, OK?

We will put to use some common sense, philosophy, physics, metaphysics and a bit of medicine in our discussion.

("Metaphysics" means "beyond physics"; it explains notions that are currently unknown, or known but not acknowledged, by official science.) Additionally, how about getting some help from the greatest minds of humanity? A number of their quotes are scattered around the book.

The two main messages of the book are:

Love, God and electromagnetic energy are all the same thing.

Romantic love is a rainbow, and you've got to taste all of its colours.

In chapter 1 and 4, we will explore the first message; in chapters 2 and 3, the second, though inevitably there will be overlaps.

We will also learn what is the point of one's existence, discover the design and the purpose of the universe, find out how to maintain passion in a long-term relationship, how to discover one's soulmate, and experience the highest levels of passion pleasures.

Why do we love sex so much? What is the purpose of your life? Who is God, and where is He? Those seemingly unrelated questions are all united by the same intrinsic human phenomenon that is known to us a "romantic love".

Romantic love – what is it? Hard to define, but those who knew it never forget it; those who lost it long to find it again. It's an irresistible emotion, both complex and intense.

His eyes across the room are MINE; I swim in them – there is no barrier. I don't know what it's called but it just flows – from him to I. I wonder – what's his name…?

You can always spot a woman in love, that temporary type of lucid beauty… Her eyes are focused and she is gazing inwards… lips curved in the subtlest of smiles… She radiates the world's unknown, and the aura that shields her makes you move away when you pass her by... You feel that she cannot be accidentally touched.

They say that sex is crude: the body fluids...! Crude...?

The morning dew on your eyelashes met by my tongue, the tenderest force; my supple curves, the hills you climb, your fingers desperately lost. You want to learn my many gazes – unyielding shields... then pastel sweet... We'll die one day, but your embraces, each one of them, I want to keep.

Dear Friend, now that we've reminded ourselves what romantic love is like, we will learn how everything in the universe works and then return to the subject of love.

To explain the universe, we will consider the concepts of structure, function and energy.

First – energy.

If you want to find the secrets of the universe, think in terms of energy, frequency and vibration.

– Nikola Tesla

The universe is made up from an infinite number of *entities (systems)*, each with the pertinent amount of energy.

Every entity could be regarded as a pendulum with its own *natural frequency* that vibrates (i.e., moves away from its starting position and returns to the latter); the number of such cycles is defined by the amount of energy available within the system.

Please visualise a child on the swings, or a dangling rod of a grandfather clock – it's like that; also see figure 1.

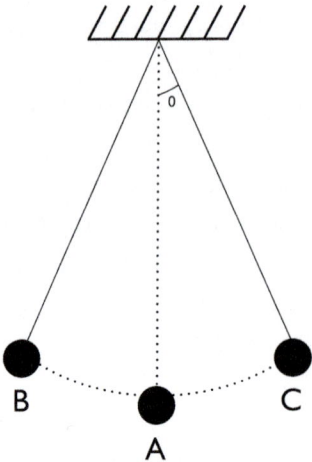

Figure 1. A simple pendulum

Every vibrating system produces waves. Waves are vibrations or disturbances that travel from one point to another, transferring energy, without transporting the matter or the medium itself. The shape of each wave is characterised by peaks and troughs. The distance between two adjacent peaks is the same as the distance between two adjacent troughs. This distance is called *wave cycle* and is measured in metres – please see figure 2.

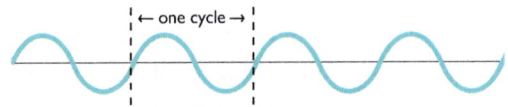

Figure 2. A wave cycle

The *period* of a wave is the amount of time it takes for a wave to complete one cycle; it is measured in time units such as seconds. The *frequency* of a wave is the number of waves produced by a source each second; it is measured in hertz, or cycles per second.

For any wave, the larger the amplitude, and the higher the frequency, the more energy the wave carries.

Natural frequency of a system (frequency of unforced vibrations) is the frequency with which the pendulum moves when left well alone.

If a force is applied to a system periodically – a *periodic force* – such as a pendulum being pulled – then there are two possible scenarios.

First scenario. The frequency of the external force is different to the pendulum's natural frequency. In this case, the pendulum will not sway far – points B and C are not far from point A; in other words, the amplitude of the pendulum's vibrations will be small. If you pushed a child on a swing randomly, you might nearly stop him swinging, for the frequency of his movements, and those of your hand, will have differed.

Second scenario. The frequency of the external force matches the system's natural frequency. In this case, the pendulum absorbs the energy from the external force and starts vibrating with a larger amplitude; points B and C are quite far from point A. This phenomenon is called *resonance*. It is interesting to note that even small periodic forces, applied at resonance frequency, can produce large amplitude vibrations. This is because the system stores vibrational energy. The well-known example is this: soldiers crossing a long bridge must "break stride" or not march in unison, to prevent the resonance between their stride and the natural frequency of the bridge's vibrations. If they don't, and resonance does occur, the power of their feet will destroy the bridge!

Depending on the point of view, every entity could be seen as a periodic force in relation to other entities, and vice versa. Also, a number of entities could be considered together as one system, a subsystem, part of the different systems simultaneously, etc. This implies that the quantity of possible interactions, and hierarchies, is infinite.

Now, let us start analysing human as one of the entities of the universe. A human is a highly complex being, but we could choose to consider him simply – a form of life with a number of natural frequencies, each representing an important aspect of his behaviour.

For example, a keen swimmer or a book reader will spend a lot of his time/life energy on swimming or book reading, respectively. Swimming/book reading behaviour would then be some of his natural frequencies.

As intimated above, the entity's energy is related to the frequency and amplitude of its vibrations. Additionally, the entity's energy is affected by its ability to self-repair effectively. The systems that are better at self-balancing, or self-repair, have the greatest number of wave cycles/the longest life duration.

In the case of a human, or another form of life, survival of the fittest implies being good at self-balancing.

Let us summarise what we've said so far. The universe consists of a number of entities, characterised by their natural frequencies, that produce waves, or vibrations, according to the latter. Every entity interacts with all the other entities – for there are no boundaries on an atomic level. The essence of exchange is interaction between entities' vibrations. Everything in the universe is thus connected *in space* via means of energy exchange – as the waves are the carriers of energy. When an entity's lifespan comes to an end/the energy within the system becomes critically low, and its remnants become parts of something else (everything is *connected in time*). An example of connection in time could be the legacy of a great artist that lives on for centuries, nurturing minds of new generations… or a pile of composting vegetable peelings that is helping your garden plants to sustain their lives.

Dear Friend, please note that connection between all entities, both in space and in time, implies the most efficient use of space and energy.

Whilst the number of interactions between the entities is infinite, each entity is most affected by/aware of the resonance level of interactions; the energy value of all the others is insignificant in comparison.

Going back to our human, he has a resonance level of interactions with other entities involved in the swimming/book reading behaviour.

Next, let us work out what is the structure of everything in the universe.

All objects are made from the same chemical elements and have common structure as the math defines objects' 3D characteristics that ensure the best use of space and access to the energy source (math terms such as Fibonacci numbers, golden ratio, golden spiral, etc. apply). This is true for an atom, a human body, a plant, a riverbed, a galaxy – all that exists works according to the universal law referred to above and summarised below. For an instant visual effect of the law at work, see the images on the next page.

Figure 3. Galaxy formation
Credit: ESO/WFI (Optical); MPIfR/ESO/APEX/A.Weiss et al.
(Submillimetre); NASA/CXC/CfA/R.Kraft et al. (X-ray)

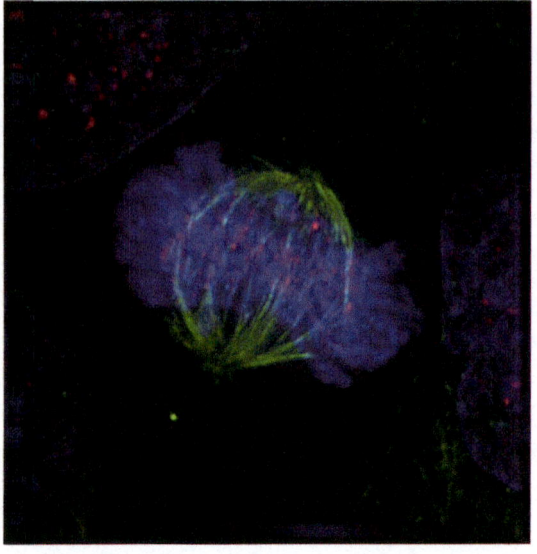

Figure 4. Metaphase (new cell formation)

Figure 5. The flow of water in the riverbed

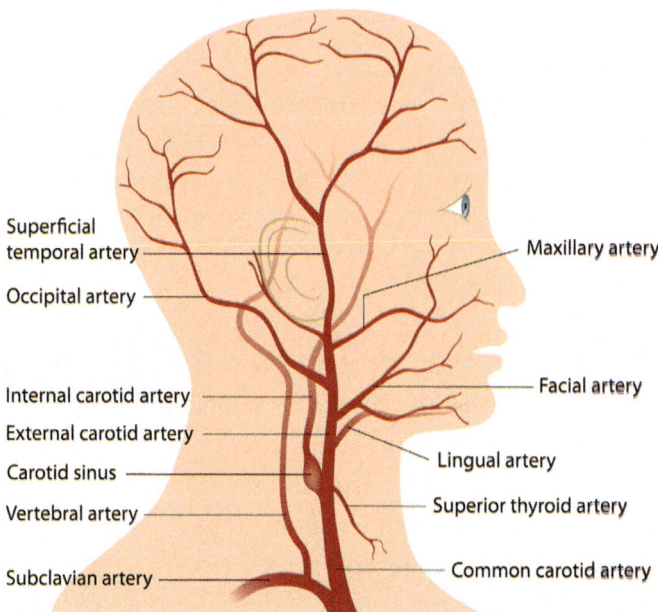

Figure 6. The flow of blood within blood vessels

The *function?* Very straightforward. Everything functions according to its natural frequencies.

Dear Friend, we are now ready to formulate the law of the universe that explains how EVERYTHING works.

The Law of the Universe: Everything is made from the same components with a common structure, everything functions according to its natural frequencies, everything has a property of self-balancing and is connected to everything else (both in space and in time) via means of energy exchange.

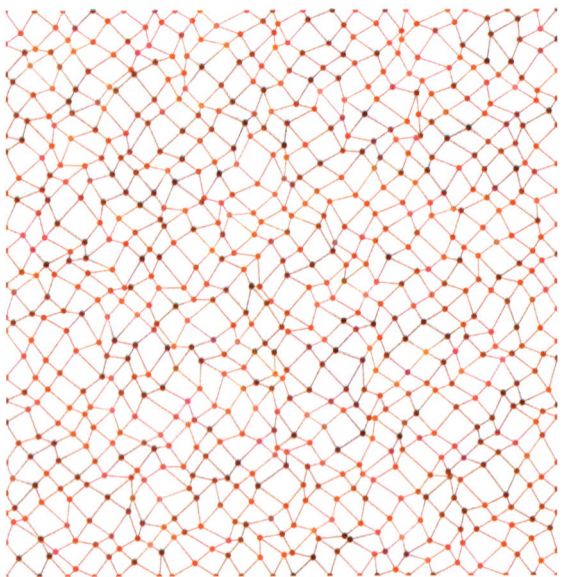

Figure 7. The energy mesh of the universe

The image above (figure 7) schematically represents the mesh, which is the energy flow between all entities within the universe (the latter are shown as the red and grey dots within the mesh). Those entities include both forms or life and inanimate objects.

But what/who orchestrates the energy exchange? In what direction, when and how much of the latter is moved between all the entities?

And what is the essence of this moving energy?
Here is what Socrates thought:

Love is a moving energy which causes us to travel toward wisdom, goodness and the beautiful. Love is the primeval cosmic desire, the spirit which moves between the gods and people linking us all and giving birth to that which becomes ultimate and eternal. Love is that which transcends from the individual to the universal bringing us spiritual inspiration and the great motivation of divine madness.

And also:

God, from a beautiful necessity, is Love.

– Martin Farquhar Tupper

What is stated in the quotes above is echoed by various religious studies, where God and love are terms often used interchangeably.

Could it then be that "love" and "spirit" and "God" all refer to the same phenomenon – the moving energy? The energy that moves within living beings and within all the other parts of the universe.

LOVE: YOUR CONNECTION WITH THE UNIVERSE

Take away love and our earth is a tomb.

– Robert Browning

Dear Friend, what entities is the universe composed of? Some of them are alive – humans, animals, plants, aliens (?); others are inanimate objects.

Does the energy flow between all of them, or just between the forms of life?

Also, the "energy of love" – it feels like a spiritual concept, does it not? Is it purely spiritual? Could we make it tangible? Let us deliberate… also, please remember that "natural frequency" of a form of life is its "behaviour", with all of its complexity, as the example below shows.

If you are a monkey, and are picking up mangoes from the branches and then throwing them to your friends, what are you actually doing? Many things. You are feeling the pleasure of having fun with your friends, the safety of being part of a community, as well as escape from the worry of where you will sleep tonight, because your usual shelter was destroyed by last night's storm. Your friends have similar feelings to yours.

Additionally, as some of the mangoes are eaten, the seeds drop down to the soil and will create new life/new mango trees, whilst the rotting flesh from the mangoes that are left on the ground will become part of the soil's structure/help to sustain plants, etc. This way, you, the monkey, are interacting with the jungle. Finally, as you are eating mangoes, you are giving nutritional energy (and pleasure) to your body, so that your life force is replenished and your life can continue.

A monkey with a natural frequency of "mango behaviour" is therefore interacting with the universe via taking in the energy (both in the physical and emotional sense) and giving it back, too.

With human being a dominant animal, it's easy to see how he initiates and maintains the energy flow. His behaviours include interacting with other humans; other animals and plants, which he uses as sources of physical and emotional energy for himself; he alters landscapes and the atmosphere; he also gives the energy back.

Humans and all other animals are capable of initiating and maintaining the energy flow between themselves and the universe.

What about plants? They are living beings, too, albeit seemingly more passive than animals. What are their behavioural patterns?

Plants collect nutrients from the soil and are supported or diseased by the living organisms within the latter. Plants are eaten/destroyed/or nurtured by humans and other animals. Plants are sheltered/nourished or broken by the structures of the landscape, by the sun, wind and rain; this is how they both give energy to the universe and receive it back.

Plants could be seen as subservient to animals and humans, as their living conditions are altered by the latter indirectly, such as via changes in plants' living environment, as well directly – their lifespan could be shortened by them being eaten/broken down and used for shelter/fuel, etc., long before they reach their maximal, biologically defined life duration.

Nevertheless, as a form of life, plants oversee how much, and when, they use their energy. For instance, they bloom later/grow longer roots/stop self-seeding as a response to environmental changes; animals and humans are merely an additional factor in their environment – that is all. Plants' "behavioural characteristics", such as blossoming when it is warm, being dormant when it's winter, etc., are some of their natural frequencies.

Plants are initiating and maintaining the energy flow between themselves and the universe.

So humans, other animals and plants all interact with each other and other parts of the universe, via means of energy exchange, the amount and direction of which each of them controls (again, see figure 7; plants and animals and humans are the dots).

What about inanimate objects?

As per universal law, their resonance interactions occur with other entities (an equivalent of "love objects"), whose natural frequencies are the same as their own natural frequencies. But who controls this and how? In the case of inanimate objects (on a scale from an atom to a galaxy), who decides how much energy flows and in what direction?

Let us consider some examples.

Live beings interact with inanimate objects and vice versa, creating energy exchange. A monkey's hand can throw a stone, and fired-up logs keep your house warm.

Volcano eruption creates a new riverbed, and this leads to liveable conditions for animals and plants. Volcano eruptions have become more frequent since humans started contributing to climate change.

> *Earthquakes, volcanic eruptions, tsunamis and landslides are some of the additional catastrophes that climate change and its rising sea levels and melting glaciers could bring.*[1]

A changing planet alters living conditions for humans, and some animals have become extinct.

The presence of a liveable planet affects the other planets within the planetary system, owing to the fact that, once the changes to the former, inflicted by the forms of life, have reached the tipping point, this will have an effect on, for instance, gravitational dynamics within the latter.[2]

In the examples above, the interactions between inanimate objects always involve some forms of life (who are "in charge" of the energy exchange). We will discuss in some more detail the energy interactions between inanimate objects and other entities in a little while (see "How do you connect to the universe" in chapter 4).

Forms of life, with their ability to direct and quantify energy flow, according to their natural frequencies, initiate

---

1. "Global Warming", http://www.livescience.com/7366-global-warming-spurearthquakes-volcanoes.html [accessed 28 April 2024]
2. "Gravitational Dynamics", Center for Astrophysics, Harvard & Smithsonian, https://www.cfa.harvard.edu/research/topic/gravitational-dynamics [accessed 28 April 2024]

and maintain the energy flow throughout the universe. More developed forms of life (such as humans and others, currently unknown to us) are capable of making the greatest impact due to the mechanism of "romantic love", which is unique to them.

Please note that love in metaphysical sense – the moving energy between all entities – is not the same phenomenon as romantic love, but they are closely related. Please wait for this to be explained in the sections that follow.

WHAT IS THE PURPOSE OF YOUR LIFE?

Without knowing what I am and why I am here, life is impossible.

– Leo Tolstoy

An unfulfilled vocation drains the colour out of man's entire existence.

– Honoré de Balzac

Dear Friend, if you want to live a gratifying life, you need to be confident that there is a meaning to your existence. If you have not found what IS your purpose… then, just like Leo and Honoré predict, you are likely to feel dissatisfied and lacking in repose.

Lone wolf

Why am I Here?
A POEM

I am a man, I want to change the world! ... no, not a "want." I NEED to! This sacred fire in my soul, it can't be wasted; that I know.
Which role is mine? Those men in charge – what monsters! And what fools! "To serve all parties" – not for me; but what am I to do? My secret terror: when I'm gone, no one will notice...
My darling – you, still here... still with me;
me – the hypocrite! For I keep choosing mediocrity – to pay our bills.
... Your face is alight with your dark burning eyes, and yet you fear stagnation.
Your smile reveals so fine a soul, your gaze such proud spirit!
You know, well, all you need to do is find the secret pass... that leads to the highest rock;
Climb on, away from all! Me, by your side...
breathe pure country air, whilst talking to your soul.
And all the answers she will give you;
Then... your evening melancholy, a washed abundantly with vine – it will be banished –
By tranquil and candid... so precious... peace of mind...
Still not enough? You need advice? Your muse can make you smile:
First make it simmer, close the lid, take it off the heat;
Now – relax and wait...
for this is how the best soups are made! Societies are controlled.
You are a MAN – but don't be on your own.

Dear Friend, what is the reason you exist? It is unique for each one of us, but the common thread seems to be helping/serving other humans.

The best way to find yourself is to lose yourself in the service of others.

– Mahatma Gandhi

Only a life lived for others is a life worthwhile.

– Albert Einstein

But how to find your purpose? You simply need to identify something you are really good at; a job you love doing – it will come to you easily, right…? Hmm… possibly not. In truth, it is onerous, impossible even, to find your purpose all by yourself (as if you live all alone, on an island). We tend to require another human being/beings to act as our mirror, to discover both our powers and our frailties. The person who is most suited to the role of being our mirror is our lover (for more details on this, please see "The role or romantic love" and "The power of romantic love" in chapter 2).

The purpose of your life is to find your own unique place within the universe's pool of energy and to interact with everything around you until the energy runs out; your place within the mesh (see figure 7 – you are one of the dots) is defined by your "loves" or your natural frequencies.

Let us explain this, and keep in mind that there are no good or bad things in nature; nature is neutral and indifferent.

Nature is not cruel, only pitilessly indifferent.

– Richard Dawkins

Therefore, the usual human understanding of love being positive and good-feeling and actions towards something, or someone, is bound to be in conflict with nature. Let us think of love as a "neutral force".

A very simple system, such as a mechanical pendulum, has only one natural frequency.

More complex entities – for example, human beings – have a number of natural frequencies, a few of which are the most important ones for any given human.

For example, if you love biking, dream of writing a book on biking routes through the Highlands of Scotland and you love your job as a teacher, but you loath your noisy neighbour, what does it practically mean? It means you will willingly spend a lot of time and energy on all of the above. It also means you'll become knowledgeable on the subjects of biking, teaching and your neighbour's noise activities, for you understand those subjects very well. They form a big part of your consciousness, where they exist – you are "giving them life" in this sense. You are also giving them life in a literal sense – for having plenty of attention from something or someone has an energy-giving, life-promoting effect.

The life duration and energy levels of every living being are limited by their biological characteristics; therefore, using the example above, you could be defined as a "form of life that is a knowledgeable expert on four subjects that he spends 75% of his total life span and energy on".

Let's describe you as per universal law:

You are an entity with four main natural frequencies (biking behaviour, travel-writing behaviour, teaching behaviour, noisy-neighbour-coping behaviour).

The purpose of your life is to interact with everything around you via energy exchange until the energy runs out.

Your most significant resonance interactions are with other entities with whom you share the same natural frequencies.

(Please note that resonance frequency is the same thing as

the natural frequency if one disregards damping, which is any factor that restricts the vibration.)

Most of your energy is spent on your resonance interactions (as resonance implies high amplitude waves hence high energy), which define the main directions of energy flow between you and the universe. Subconsciously or not, you are controlling your energy – the direction of its flow and the quantity of energy within the flow.

Please note that some of your natural frequencies could change during your life – for example, those related to your hobbies.

The natural frequency related to your "dream", your "life mission" stays the same; or rather it develops during your life, and different people become aware of it at different ages. (In the example above, "life mission" is becoming a travel writer.)

Your natural frequency related to your "romantic love" is the same as your "life mission" natural frequency and is the highest natural frequency amongst all the other natural frequencies that characterise you as an entity. This will be explained further in chapter 2, in the section "The role of romantic love".

WHAT IS THE PURPOSE OF THE UNIVERSE?

For small creatures such as we the vastness is bearable only through love.

– Carl Sagan

Dear Friend, we can easily relate to what Carl says, can't we? The universe seems to consist of an infinite number of planets, ours is the only one we know, and it's anyone's guess how many friendly or belligerent species occupy the rest of them. However, let's not panic. We have already deduced that the essence of the universe is love, haven't we?

On the other hand... the universe is full of death and aggression, is it not? This is how humanity behaves; this is the essence of the biological pyramid/food chain. The stars, which give birth to their families of planets... a few billion years later, they engulf them, digest and scatter the remnants into the interstellar medium, so that the cycle can start all over again.

Dear Friend, in the paragraphs above, can you spot a pattern? The universe is filled with love which feels positive to us; the universe is filled with violence which feels negative to us. If you combine the positive and the negative, what you get is a neutrality – the universe has no "feelings".

Once again, Carl helps us to work things out:

The universe seems neither benign nor hostile, merely indifferent.

– Carl Sagan

Speaking in neutral terms, and keeping the law of the universe in mind, we could state that the universe is a space filled with energy. It needs to make sure that there is enough space for all entities and enough energy for all entities.

The most efficient use of space is ensured by the 3D characteristics of all the objects complying with mathematical constants (as explained above), as well as having a great variety of entities, apt to filling all the empty spaces.

What about the most efficient use of energy? How does the universe provide for that?

Firstly, energy flows between the systems (entities) within any given moment of time (connection in space); also, the remnants of the expired systems are being reused within other systems (connection in time); this way, energy never disappears.

Secondly, the systems with the most effective self-balancing prevail.

The purpose of the universe is to exist for as long as the energy within doesn't run out and both space and energy are being used most efficiently.

HOW DOES THE UNIVERSE WORK: IN DETAIL

When a man's knowledge is not in order, the more of it he has, the greater will be his confusion.

– Herbert Spencer

In the first few pages of this book, we have considered how the universe works via metaphysical, philosophical deliberations. We now will proceed with explaining the law of the universe from the physics perspective.

According to the currently accepted physics definition, there are four primary forces that exist in nature – gravitational, electromagnetic, weak and strong nuclear forces. They are deemed to govern the way atoms and planets behave – and all the other objects whose size is in between. Without going into details, the complicated descriptions of all those, seemingly separate, forces, take up dozens of pages of textbooks!

Dear Friend, you and I could try a simpler approach – we will summarise it in four paragraphs that follow – just as Albert advises.

If you can't explain it simply you don't understand it well enough. The grand aim of all science is to cover the greatest number of empirical facts by logical deduction from the smallest number of hypothesis or axioms.

– Albert Einstein

As per universal law, every entity in the universe vibrates (produces waves), and every vibrating system (entity) interacts with everything else. Amongst all the interactions, those that cause resonance are the most significant ones.

Mechanical resonance refers to the most significant interactions between all entities' vibrations that are produced at a level larger than atom. Electromagnetic resonance refers to the most significant interactions between all entities' vibrations that are produced on an atomic scale. Nuclear resonance refers to the most significant interactions between all entities' vibrations that are produced within the nuclei of the atoms.

Therefore, all four forces referred to above are simply subtypes of one force (let's call it force X) that are considered at different levels: larger than atom; atom; nucleus inside the atom.

The essence of force X is interaction between the waves, or vibrations, that are produced by all entities. Force X is most significant with resonance-type interactions.

Interactions between all entities on the atomic level are called "electromagnetic waves", which carry electromagnetic energy. Every form or life and every inanimate object emits electromagnetic energy. Every form of life and every inanimate object interact with each other via their electromagnetic waves.

(Please note that the reason we are not discussing here force X at the level larger than atom, and force X at the level of the nucleus is this: the former is only significant for very large objects (such as celestial bodies), and the latter is only significant for very small entities, the order of the size of the nucleus inside the atom. On the other hand, force X at an atomic level – electromagnetic radiation – is applicable to all the objects that are part of an ordinary human's life.)

Do you remember – we've concluded that force X is "love, God, spirit"?

On an atomic level, force X is also known as "electromagnetic energy".

LOVE: METAPHYSICAL AND HUMAN

> *The world is not comprehensible, but it is embraceable: through the embracing of one of its beings.*
>
> – Martin Buber

Dear Friend, what we have discussed in the sections above, love being a moving energy, a spirit within living beings, God – does it feel intuitively the same as, or different to, "love towards a person" or "romantic love"? Let us consider the link between the two.

Love being a moving energy could be visualised as an infinite net that is covering an entire universe. Love towards a person inspires you to "pull" the energy net in a direction of your want, to bring about the results you desire for your loved one.

A human has many different "loves", or favourite behaviours, which energetically link him to the universe. However, his romantic life and related activities are of special importance, as this is what he spends most of his time and energy on; it's his number-one priority. (Dear Friend, do you disagree? Please wait until we discuss this further in chapter 2, in the sections "The role of romantic love" and "The power of romantic love".)

> *Love is the strongest of the passions. In all the others, desires have to adapt themselves to cold reality, but in love, realities obligingly rearrange themselves to conform with desire. From the moment he falls in love, even the wisest man no longer sees anything as it really is.*
>
> – Stendhal, *Love*

And now we have come to a controversial point. Can the universe really "afford" for everyone to fall in love at the same time? If a human is one of the strongest influencers of the energy flow, and he cannot see the reality in the state of love, it would create chaos in the energy ocean of the universe. Imagine everyone pulling the energy net in different directions (and with the greatest determination!) all at the same time; it can't happen – it doesn't happen. The universe seems to have allocated the right time, and a different time, for all of us.

> *Man is not free to avoid doing what gives him greater pleasure than any other action. Love is like a fever, which comes and goes quite independently of the will.*
>
> – Stendhal, *Love*

This observation that a human "cannot control it" simply means that several collateral circumstances all need to come together for you to be ready to fall in love.

Rephrasing this in a metaphysical sense, the right time for you to fall in love is exactly the time when the energy field of the universe that surrounds you is ready for a major shake-up; because this is exactly what you will do, when in love. Reciprocally, your own life will experience quite a turbulence when you are in love.

See figure 8 for the visual effect:

Figure 8

The summits of the "energy mountains" in figure 8 correspond to the places where a person in love is.

To summarise, romantic love towards another person refers to a natural frequency on which a human will spend most of his energy, and, correspondingly, the energy of the universe will be most affected by this type of connection. (We will discuss this in greater detail in chapter 4, in the section "Eternal".)

HAPPINESS: METAPHYSICAL AND HUMAN

We can easily forgive a child who is afraid of the dark; the real tragedy of life is when men are afraid of the light.

– Plato

I think we risk becoming the best-informed society that has ever died of ignorance.

– Rubén Blades

Why are so many modern humans unhappy? Could the main reason be this? Whilst being a part of nature, humans behave like they are not; we seem to have decided that we are "above nature". But this is simply an illusion; just because you "decide" not to be a part of nature, you do not alter the fact that you are. Confucius agrees.

Mankind differs from the animals only by a little and most people throw that away.

– Confucius

Humans invented behavioural patterns that do not exist in nature. Let us discuss three main ones.

1. Modern society demands that male and female roles are identical.

Dear Friend, do you think that a man and a woman are the same? Or do you agree with the opinions expressed below?

The worst form of equality is to try to make unequal things equal.

— Aristotle

Man can never be woman's equal in the spirit of selfless service with which nature has endowed her.

— Mahatma Gandhi

The simplest of women are wonderful liars who could extricate themselves from the most difficult dilemmas with a skill bordering on genius.

— Guy de Maupassant

Men are by nature merely indifferent to each other, but women are by nature enemies.

— Arthur Schopenhauer

A man's face is his autobiography. A woman's face is her work of fiction.

— Oscar Wilde

2. An attitude of waste and excess. Humans destroy the plants/animals that they don't intend to eat/kill animals that do not endanger their life.

3. Humans invented "morals" that do not exist in nature. Being part of nature, humans possess behavioural instincts in relation to the entire spectrum of the animal behaviour but are not able to apply them, as the morals/or modern society ways demand for them to be suppressed.

Corresponding animals' behavioural patterns are as follows:

1. Female and male roles are well defined and are never the same.

2. Within the human free ecosystem, there is space for a number of species to co-exist, with predators and resource availability being the main control factors.

3. Nature users every tool of the behavioural spectrum to ensure survival.

Please note that behavioural patterns of animals, described above, lead to an efficient use of space and energy – no waste, no empty space – in accordance with the universal law, whilst the behaviour of humans violates that very law.

Please also note that the attitude of "no waste, no empty space" is, in essence, the same thing as "the attitude of love", encouraged by all religions and spiritual teachings.

If you choose to not destroy the plant that you don't intend to eat/and not to kill the insect that doesn't endanger your life/practice peaceful and friendly behaviour towards other humans who are not an immediate threat to your life/livelihood, you are showing them love – giving them a chance to take up their space within the universal pool of energy.

Rephrasing the above in metaphysical terms: happiness means that all entities are given space, energy and interconnectedness.

In human terms: if you want to be happy, you need to

accept that you are part of nature and practice as many natural behavioural patterns as possible.

At the same time, you are obliged to recognise that at the current stage of human evolution, your life is subject to a contemporary set of modern society/moral obligations that restrict your access to all possible behavioural patterns and so you need to adjust your behaviour accordingly.

In addition to the overall attitude of love described above, if you are a human, you also seem to need to be happy in a romantic love sense (see more in "The formula of passion" in chapter 3) in order to feel happy overall.

CHAPTER 2

The Anatomy of Love

THE ROLE OF ROMANTIC LOVE

All my life, my heart has yearned for a thing I cannot name.

– Andre Breton

Love is man's and woman's deepest need. It's not the threat of illness or poverty that crushes human spirit, but the fear that there is no one who truly cares; no one who really understands.

– Linda Goodman

Dear Friend, does your heart assent to what Andre and Linda say? And did you wonder why the person who "truly cares and understands" is your lover and no one else?

Let us do a quick analysis here.

Your family members: they are a big part of the reason for your emotional pains and/or should be sheltered from knowing the depth of your unhappiness.

Your friends – yes, they could give you love and support, but this has its limits. Even best friends don't have endless patience, are often envious of us or just way too busy with their own lives. If you mistreat your friend, repeatedly, she will not stay with you; your lover might.

Rare as is true love, true friendship is rarer.

– Jean de La Fontaine

Romantic love does encompass a kaleidoscope of feelings and emotions (as we will be discussing shortly), however, a big part of it is "being one" with your beloved, which maximises patience, minimises envy, and gives you a huge incentive for seeking and maintaining their happiness.

Our entire lives – including the choice of profession, the choice of where to live, etc. – are centred around our search for love. We might be immediately aware of it or only recognise it in retrospect. Why is romantic love so important for us humans? Let us consider what are the main needs of a human animal and other animals and compare them.

Two main needs are shared by humans and other animals: the need to procreate and rear the young; to live according to one's natural frequencies.

But it is more complicated for us, in four different ways.

Firstly, there is a great possible variety of natural frequencies, and endless possible combinations of the latter, different for every human, whilst for animals, they are much alike, within the same species.

Secondly, when rearing the young, animals of each species will do it in the same way, whilst there will be a great variation in how humans' young are brought up. Moreover, the long-term health and well-being of a human is significantly affected by the quality of the parenting that he experienced.

Thirdly, it is much harder to be a healthy human than to be a healthy animal. If you are an animal and have shelter and food and no predator shortens your life, you are fine. If you are a human, your physical health depends on your mental health, and the latter is subject to your upbringing and the quality of your subsequent relationships, and other factors… plus all the above are intricately interwoven.

The fourth, and perhaps the most important, difference is related to the advanced intellectual and spiritual development pertinent to humans, in comparison with other animals.

Every human feels an intense urge to achieve his unique potential, to carry out his life's mission, and this is a natural frequency that is unique for every single human. With lower-intellect animals, this phenomenon doesn't seem to exist at all.

Its due to those four differences that humans have an additional need – the third main need, perhaps the strongest of all – the thirst for romantic love, owing to the fact that we sense that if we are mated to a person who is truly close to us, our chances of rearing our young into healthy, happy adults, being healthy and happy adults ourselves, as well as finding our life's mission and carrying it out in the best possible way are the greatest. (Please see more on this subject in the section "Love and marriage".)

We feel that we are incomplete without that special person; and being "half" of something feels very uncomfortable – hence an unquenchable crave to meet them and be with them.

> *Man and Woman are inseparable. Each is an equal part of the other. The circle (O) represents Eternity, for it symbolizes the Serpent, eating its own tail. From the masculine (positive) head of the Serpent flows the male-positive energy force into female (negative) tail of the serpent. Simultaneously, from the tail of the Serpent flows the female (negative) energy into the Serpent's head.*
>
> *– Linda Goodman, Love Signs*

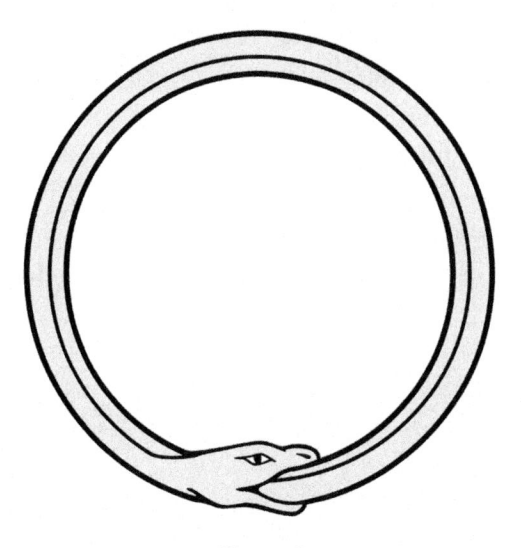

Figure 9

To summarise, the role of romantic love is to help us carry out our life's mission; rear our young into healthy, happy people, and to make us healthy and happy.

FALL IN LOVE AND STAY IN LOVE

> *Blessed is the influence of one true, loving human soul on another.*
>
> – George Eliot

Dear Friend, as you probably know, it is quite easy to fall in love, but to maintain that feeling long-term seems to be a challenge. Let us find out how we can perpetuate the wonderful "I am in love!" state.

From the previous chapter, we know that romantic love's frequency is the most important natural frequency for any human – he will willingly give it the largest portion of his life's energy allowance. The energy of waves is directly proportionate to their frequency. Therefore, amongst all natural frequencies that a human has, the frequency related to romantic love is the highest. Let's call it the main natural frequency.

Apart from the energy aspect of it, what makes it a main frequency is this: main natural frequency relates to a unique essence of any given human's spirit, and it is this essence that makes a human choose both his life mission and his romantic love.

Jasmine

Falling in love

When we fall in love, we become capable of adapting our main natural frequency to that of our lover; this makes for high-energy-level resonance interactions – which is also known as "the honeymoon period". Beyond this stage, we realise that our main natural frequencies are not the same (as they are unique for each human), and this might feel like falling out of love.

To achieve lasting romantic love with another person, your main natural frequencies need to become the same. This happens when you reach a perfect harmony between your physical, emotional and spiritual natures.

Developing this harmony could take months or years – depending on the couple. In parallel, your life missions will become clear to both of you, and more likely than not, they will be complementary. Once the same natural frequency is reached, your union will produce the highest, maximum energy levels you are biologically capable of. This is for two reasons. The romantic love frequency is the highest, as explained above, and the amplitude is the highest because of the resonance between the both of you.

When in the highest energy state, you will experience "transcendence", which refers to the most pleasurable lovemaking there is. In parallel, the universe will benefit from the high-energy deeds that you will carry out.

So it all sounds wonderful, right? The highest levels of pleasure; the perfect harmony; in love forever… but it might take… years? FORGET IT!

The tragedy of a modern human is that we are all about "now!"; the immediate relief and the instant satisfaction.

ONE-NIGHT STAND? NO THANK YOU!

Economic progress, in capitalist society, means turmoil.

– Joseph A. Schumpeter

Our modern world is so restless; so very complicated. This complexity is all wrong; it feels too much, and it is hurting us in many ways. Simple mind-numbing measures are an antidote we use. Alcohol, one-night stands, drugs, etc.

A "one-night stand" is very basic; it's what animals do – it doesn't matter who they mate with, as long as he is a specimen of the same species. Our overstretched and foggy minds, confused and sore hearts, switched off – it's a respite! It's only the body – shock it! Yes, risky... but it does feels nice...

Is it a good thing then? Harmless? Maybe not.

Like any other "shock therapy", the benefits are instant; the ill effects – long-term; recovery rate – variable. It destroys something precious inside us, as detailed in the section "The colour black" (see chapter 3).

In terms of the instant benefit, it is only partial; the level of contentment we feel from such an encounter is insufficient. This is because you are "mating" with a person who has a different natural frequency, which mean no resonance will occur. Correspondingly, the energy level of your encounter will be low, and so will be your perceived pleasure.

Accidentally, "porn" could be defined as a cinematic equivalent of a one-night stand; and the huge revenue it generates serves as proof of our need for a calming antidote, and our thirst for love, of which porn is one of the "ready to eat" surrogates.

(Please note that in the discussion above, we have referred to the intentional, recurrent pastime of using another person "as a piece of flesh" that many modern humans partake in; they click on your profile similar to the way they'd order a pizza. Occasionally, a random sexual encounter could lead to a meaningful relationship, or be a one-off positive influence, but this tends to be an exception.)

Dark Cave
A POEM

This cave is black... dark, squelching place... we, all in here, naked
The penetrating pungent scent... chaos of fire, overflowing... he is in my mouth... who? Who cares...
It's just not real, none of it!... so nothing is off limits... the gurgling lust... is choking us...
... the instant hands... debased embrace...

His heaving thighs... I can resist... oh no, I can't...! It's nature's call... I'm weak...
The delving stinger trembles...
He's drinking me... in every way... oh, how I love that he's brave...
I, Piece of Meat, belong to all...
It's you – tonight; the coarse delight

I've made you drunk... I've dried you up...
It's cold... it hurts!... the worms in me... I want to see the sun!
The spasms, the jerks, the salty taste...
NO – I don't want to see your face; I'm done.

Good-byyeeee...! You leave my mind... my soul has left the cave.

Dear Friend, many of us feel that simplified forms of "love" have an important place in the modern world. Be it a one-night stand, or a number of short-term relationships… we keep changing lovers, for we don't feel satisfied in how it feels to be with them… they don't smother our insupportable disquiet.

Why is that? The last words of the poem above crystallise it – don't you think? "My soul has left the cave."

Whatever the duration, or the particular nature of your "love relationship", if the deep, soul-to-soul connection has not been developed, the union will not endure.

THE QUESTION OF A SOULMATE

He's more myself than I am. Whatever our souls are made of, his and mine are the same.

– Emily Brontë, *Wuthering Heights*

Dear Friend, you are probably aware of a popular notion that there is just one, only one person in the whole world (a few billion people…) who is perfect for you, and you could never be quite as happy with anyone else, so you better hope to find him (or her). Could this really be so?

From a metaphysical point of view, nothing could be further from the truth. Think about it: humans (and other high-intelligence forms of life) are capable of making the greatest impact on the universe; their ability to carry out their "mission" is dependent on finding their romantic love, and the chance of this happening is about one in a billion!.

The universe would want to facilitate just the opposite: make it possible for a human to be romantically fulfilled with a great number of possible mates, to make sure it definitely happens.

Dear Friend, you might or might not believe in astrology, and the discussion of that beautiful ancient science is not a subject of this book. But you are probably familiar with astrological concepts of dividing humans into different personality types and offering compatibility suggestions.

One of the greatest modern astrologers, Linda Goodman, stipulates that a person could live contentedly, and with ease, with someone who is "compatible" with them.

However, the spiritual heights of the sort of love that poets write about are unlikely to be experienced that way. It appears that the thunderbolt level of energy, the pain and pleasures of deep passion, occur as a result of "not very compatible" people learning how to connect in the most intimate ways, altering each other in the process.

Why is this the case, do you think?

Firstly, we are instinctively attracted to someone who is quite dissimilar, because mixing different gene pools maximises the health of the potential offspring.

Secondly, the "Beauty and the Beast" or the "bad boy" phenomenon implies that lovers are helping each other to become their best self, which is an important aspect of a love relationship, encouraged in every culture and by every religion (see more in the section "The power of a romantic love").

In astrological terms, for the Bull and a Goat to love, for Lion and Ram to love, is nearly effortless. But for a Ram to achieve harmony with the Crab; for Lion with the Scorpion; the Bull with a water bearer – these demonstrate a higher love.

– Linda Goodman, *Love Signs*

Accidentally, if you have attained such a deep spiritual, emotional and physical union with your lover, you might well feel that he is "the one, and the only one". But this is probably because a human being simply cannot handle more than one relationship of such an intensity in one lifetime, and not because such a love could not have been attained with someone else.

If you consider a variety of prospective lovers, the nature of your dance will be different with each of them, and some moves could be much more gruelling than others... but you will surely get there – just as long as you persist.

> *We waste time looking for the perfect lover, instead of creating the perfect love.*
>
> – Tom Robbins

THE POWER OF ROMANTIC LOVE

> *The cure for all the ills and wrongs, the cares, the sorrows, and the crimes of humanity, all lie in the one word "love". It is the divine vitality that everywhere produces and restores life.*
>
> – Lydia M. Child

(If you like, you could listen to the following piece of classical music as a soundtrack to the section that follows: Pyotr Ilyich Tchaikovsky, Romeo and Juliet *(Overture-Fantasy))*

Dear Friend, in the previous section, we have discovered that the role of romantic love is to help us carry out our love's mission, to rear healthy and capable offspring, and to make us both healthy and happy. This does sound great, but what, specifically, do we have to do? Let us work it out.

When you are in love, you are trying to be your best self. And your lover will be wanting to do the same. This way, love helps every person to improve themselves.

Additionally, being full of energy, and feeling positive and powerful, usually means productive and positive activities are being carried out, so the world around us profits.

Sustaining the wonderful state of being in love, as described above, is a different matter.

Let's analyse what tends to happen. Once we stop being "on our best behaviour", we inevitably show to each other our unlovable qualities. And learning to love the unlovable is a challenge that some of us find way too much, and we give up on that person... and find another person... the cycle continues. If the challenge of loving the unlovable was not a very important love lesson, why would it be immortalised in folklore? One of the examples of the latter is the story of Beauty and the Beast. The Beast's only chance to become a Prince is to find a Beauty who will love him whilst he is still a Beast.

There is no person that love cannot heal; there is no soul that love cannot save.

– Carlos Santana

Whilst fairy tales make it clear that being loved for what you are when you are unlovable changes you for the better, they omit to say that Beauty's personal qualities are altered, too – in the process of learning how to love the Beast.

To summarise, the state of being in love helps a person, and the world, to be the best they can be. Staying in love depends on learning how to love the unlovable; once mastered, this leads to further emotional and spiritual development of both parties.

For some people, they mostly "fall in love with their head"; they appreciate a person's looks, professional and other status, and decide that person is a "good catch". On further acquaintance, getting to know someone's personality, loving with one's intellect only could continue, as they are calmly assessing and scrutinising their lover's qualities.

Even when her beautiful blue eyes seem to gaze at me with least restraint, I can always read in them a cold, malevolent scrutiny. Is it possible that this is love?

– Stendhal, *Scarlet and Black*

Falling in love with your heart is a deeper, and more genuine, passion; this often means "loving against your better judgement", just like Émile and Victor observe:

He knew she was foolish, foul and a liar, but he desired her all the same.

– Émile Zola, *Nana*

The inexplicable fact is that the blinder love is, the more tenacious it is. It is never stronger than when it is completely unreasonable.

– Victor Hugo

You always choose the lover who loves you against their own judgement; you intuitively know that this is the best love there is.

The greatest happiness of life is the conviction that we are loved; loved for ourselves, or rather, loved in spite of ourselves.

– Victor Hugo

It's not just the negatives you can see in your darling, if you love them with your heart. You can actually experience an ethereal feeling of "seeing a God in them". It's hard to describe what it is… a kind of awareness… a glimpse of "goodness" or "truth" that you perceive shining in their face during that moment, for example, when they are helping a friend/caring for a child, etc. The quote below describes this so beautifully:

> *When you love a man, he becomes more than a body. His physical limbs expand, and his outline recedes, vanishes. He is rich and sweet and right. He is part of the world, the atmosphere, the blue sky and the blue water.*
>
> – Gwendolyn Brooks

If you can learn to love both with your head and your heart, you will then see your lover very clearly, with all their strengths and weaknesses; and none of us can see ourselves that way.

> *Love is when he gives you a piece of your soul, that you never knew was missing.*
>
> – Torquato Tasso

You are practically becoming your loved one's "spiritual mirror", and this way you help them to find out what is their life's mission and how to accomplish it.

You will be able to love the unlovable only if you engage both your head and your heart.

For example, your lover might have a negative quality of being short-tempered, impolite and, at times, physically violent. With your head you can understand that this behaviour stems from his unfortunate childhood. With your heart, you can feel compassion and forgiveness, and this will help him to successfully conquer his demons.

Whilst both lovers learn to love the unlovable, their roles are not identical.

Please consider the opinions of two philosophers; one epitomises Eastern culture; another the Western one. They lived centuries apart – yet the quintessence of what they say is the same.

Woman is a beam of the divine Light… she is a Creator, not a creature… she establishes the esoteric sense of knowledge and guides those who attain to it. Through her perfume, we breathe paradise.

– Rumi

In everything relating to the force and energy of love, women should be the sovereigns; it is from them we hope for happiness, and they will never fail to grant us that, as soon as they can govern our hearts with intelligence.

– Lord Saint-Evremond

WILL YOU BE MY MUSE?

Women are our most miraculous muse, an enchanted intangibility that encourages all art.

– CeeLo Green

In ancient Greek religion and mythology, the Muses are the inspirational goddesses of literature, science and the arts. A muse is also someone who impels and energises a creative artist. Every man secretly wants to meet a woman who is amazing enough to be his muse. Remember the famous proverb? "Behind every successful man there stands a woman."

My Muse
A POEM

You are the air in my lungs, the light inside my soul.
I have not seen you for a week and everything feels wrong.
The moody windows of your eyes, your skin, so soft and mine
Your words provoke and challenge me... I want to laugh and cry
I never understand you – I don't know if I'd want that
I cannot live without you, please hurry and come back.

Usually, his muse is also his lover.

His male desires and his spiritual needs mingled and seemed to spring from the dark depths of his being, as though they were a single flowering from the trunk of his life.

– Émile Zola, *Nana*

Dear Friend, if you are wondering if a man could be a muse for a woman, I feel the answer is "no". This is not a competition; male and female energy are complementary. A woman enjoys being a muse, and a man enjoys having a muse – this way they are both happy.

As stated in the previous section, your need for romantic love and your desire to fulfil your life's mission are unique to you and are intrinsically linked. There is a way to be loved that will make you feel contented, and this way is unique to you. There is a mission that no other human being, but you, can accomplish.

Sadly, many of us either never find out what their mission is or are confused in how to go about achieving it, and so we feel not quite happy and never fully content, all of our lives.

Dear Friend, do you think it's possible that the tragedy of unfulfilled lives that we see in abundance in the modern world is linked to the lack of love that those individuals experience?

Learning to love with your head and your heart requires a great deal of patience and spiritual strength; this is beautifully summarised in the powerful quote that follows:

> *Love is patient, love is kind. It does not envy, it does not boast, it is not proud. It does not dishonour others, it is not self-seeking, it is not easily angered, it keeps no record of wrongs. Love does not delight in evil but rejoices with the truth. It always protects, always trusts, always hopes, always perseveres.*
>
> — 1 Corinthians 13.4–13, the Bible

Whilst all of us have the power of love within us, many of us are unable, or unwilling, to tap into it. But if you can do it – the gift of love your lover will receive will help him to accomplish his greatest ambitions and fulfil his innermost passions.

To summarise, the power of romantic love lies in teaching us to love the unlovable, and becoming our lovers' emotional and spiritual mirrors in the process. The latter empowers our lover to discover and carry out his life mission.

THE TRAGEDY OF ROMANTIC LOVE

The course of true love never did run smooth.

— William Shakespeare

(If you like, you could listen to the following piece of classical music as a soundtrack to the section that follows: Erik Satie, Gnossienne No. 1*)*

Dear Friend, the famous words above, they became a cliché; they are so true – why do you think this is the case? Perhaps because love, inherently, is full of challenges and contradictions.

The tragedy of romatic love

1. YOU NEVER FEEL THAT YOU ARE LOVED ENOUGH

If she reassures you sufficiently, this placates you, but not for long; the doubts creep in with distressing regularity, and, eventually, her patience with having to dispel your fears might start wearing thin.

> *The god of love lives in a state of need. It is a need. It is an urge. It is a homeostatic imbalance. Like hunger and thirst, it's almost impossible to stamp out.*
>
> — Plato

2. YOU FEAR FOR THE SAFETY AND WELL-BEING OF THE ONE YOU LOVE

The more you love, the more heartbroken you will be if something bad happened to her, so you are forever anxious and this might lead to your attempts to control her/restrict her lifestyle choices, which could make her cross with you.

3. YOU ARE AT ODDS WITH OTHER PEOPLE

> *Love has reasons which reason cannot understand.*
>
> — Blaise Pascal

When you see the negative qualities in a person you love, you might feel that they are perfectly excusable, for your heart knows all the complexities of her nature and life history. Others are judging her actions only with the power of reason, far inferior to the wisdom of the heart that you have developed towards her. You might even end up feeling that you are constantly needing to excuse her/justify her actions. This is exhausting, and, eventually, you might prefer to simply avoid the company of those other people. Contrarily, if she sees that you don't have other people around you, it might make her love you less, for your perceived worth/her reasons for potential jealousy could both decrease in her eyes.

4. THE CONTRARIETY

"<u>Please be near, but far.</u>" You feel that you want to be very close to the one you love; at the same time, to sustain love, you need to learn to stay away, even if you don't want to. She can only admire you if she sees you at a distance.

Once the realization is accepted that even between the closest human beings, infinite distances continue, a wonderful living side by side can grow, if they succeed in loving the distance between them which makes it possible for each to see the other whole against the sky.

– Rainer Maria Rilke

"Please hear 'yes' when I say 'no'." She is modest! She is fearless but shy… powerful but scared… she might change her mind… her mood – it can't be helped. Remember, she can never be your "friend"; she is your *sweetest enemy*.

The very essence of romance is uncertainty.

– Oscar Wilde

"I want to tell you all my secrets…! Including those I never want you to know."

We want to be infinitely close with our beloved, becoming one flesh… at the same time, we are aware that having no secrets from them makes them love us less.

Love is an endless mystery, for it has nothing else to explain it.

– Rabindranath Tagore

5. THERE IS ONLY ONE STEP BETWEEN LOVE AND HATRED
Deep trust and intimacies that lovers share imply that they know each other's innermost secrets/vulnerabilities. Extreme

care with handling that private information is required, for any accidental disclosure (that you might think is a mere trifle) might strike her as an unforgivable betrayal. Other reasons for hatred might include jealousy, envy, etc. (see this detailed in "The colour green" in chapter 3).

6. OBSTRUCTIVE COLLATERAL EVENTS/PRECARIOUS LIFE SITUATION

The latter fuel passion because they increase the potential for pain, which is an important part of love (see "The formula of passion" in chapter 3).

> *The element that characterises the dark passion: the immensity of the difficulty to be overcome and the dark uncertainty of the issue.*
>
> – Stendhal, *Scarlet and Black*

And if the challenges above make you feel like you need to be balancing on a tightrope over the abyss – yes, you actually do!

LOVE AND MARRIAGE

> *True love is like ghosts, which everyone talks about and few have seen.*
>
> – François de La Rochefoucauld

Dear Friend, from the section "The power of a romantic love", you might have concluded that there are immense benefits to a person and the world in general, if romantic love is both developed and sustained, whilst the section "The tragedy of romantic love" sheds light on the significant challenges that need to be overcome, in order to reap the benefits that love like that offers.

True love might well be as rare as ghosts – but where lasting romantic love does exist, it is usually in the context of a marriage. And this is simply because the main secret of lasting love is longstanding and unwavering commitment; and "marriage keeps you together when you fall out of love until you fall back in". When a human is attempting a huge and challenging undertaking, he rarely succeeds immediately; he has to "try and try and try again", just like Albert says below.

The art of love is largely the art of persistence.

– Albert Ellis

LOVE IS THE DRUG

Dear Friend, as already discussed in the previous sections, your sweetheart is a person who will have more time, patience, understanding and forgiveness for you than anyone else in your life ever would. Let us talk a bit more about "health benefits" that love like that offers.

Your mental health is intrinsically connected to your physical one; they cannot be regarded/treated separately – it never works.

Let us consider two obvious examples in relation to very common chronic mental illnesses: anxiety and depression. An anxious person tends to suffer from a cocktail of skin issues, chronic headaches, as well as indigestion/bowel disorders. This happens because persistent anxiety alters levels of some of your body's chemical substances/affects your nervous system. Consequently, body organs are harmed, leading to the latter diseases.

Someone who is depressed is likely to, for instance, comfort eat, and if this continues long-term, then pertinent hypertension, diabetes and heart disease are almost inevitable.

Whilst any reasonable person would *wish* to see their lover eat healthily/keep their weight within the healthy range/feel calm and positive/avoid excess alcohol, etc., "wishing" is a drop in the ocean of what your beloved one needs.

If one doesn't do all the right things, there is, typically, a complex explanation for this and a mass of hidden issues – usually rooted in one's childhood. Could professionals help? Theoretically – yes; practically – no. Thousands (!) of hours of "compassionate and highly intelligent talking therapies" is the only effective intervention, and what healthcare system could afford that? (Dear Friend, please note that this subject will be explored in great detail in the next book in the series, which will be on mental health.)

So it is down to both of you – do you love each other enough to keep healthy and to heal all the old wounds? There is a way to be loved that is perfect for you, but it might take your darling a long time to learn it. If she gives up on you, or you will lose your faith in her – oh, what a shame!

You learn to love by loving – by paying attention and doing what one thereby discovers has to be done.

– Aldous Huxley

The Galaxy of Passion
A POEM

If she's no longer slim... please don't stop loving her
her weight – it's her self-harm; her issues – deep and many
your heart... is it big enough to help her?...
She cooks and cleans for you; she kisses... still, you leave her.
She, such a fool! So kind and so naïve... for she is stroking... the totally wrong places...
The caring love, you can't – don't understand! You've never known it.
Your mother, when you were a little boy, she always left you to cry yourself to sleep
she never gave you a pet name...
... and so, the loving neural pathways...
inside your brain...
are simply not developed...
You have the other ones. Space and control – is what you crave...
She needs to... twist and turn her love, and harness it – the best she can...
and then just let you be.
Her passion... she must hide, so deep inside, the unassailable mountain...
with solid walls... her cries are hushed...
for months... for years! (Oh no, I can't survive, I won't...!)
My brain, will you just stop... my heart is talking.
She must believe that passion's treasures... they will not tarnish;
their lustre – it will deepen; the tastings of amour – delicious, dizzily cocktailed... will wait for them... inside the cave
And then one day... he'll learn to love her – in her way.

And you will buy us a house
In the galaxy of passion... on a planet of total abandon...
with the daily kissing meteorite rains
The kids and dogs, when safely away...
(Do you know those astronomers who say that supernova
explosions only happen
Two times a century in the Milky Way... they haven't done
their homework!)
Because... cause you give me one, whenever I say
As often as my cup of tea, and at least twice a day.

In a long-standing relationship, both man and woman end up "chipping off" each other's imperfections, and the process is often painful. But is it love's fault?

> *Love is blamed for all sickness of the heart. This is because love is so potent that to invite it in is to challenge all that it is not. It is our own misunderstandings, expectations and definitions that sicken us.*
>
> *– Aurora Clawson*

Marriage is encouraged in each society and by every church. For a man to keep his woman, he needs to become his best self. For a woman to keep her man, she needs to become her best self.

All human character weaknesses and misfortunes could be healed by love; in the absence of love they may result in mental health issues/broken families/criminal activities.

Love is a mutual self-giving which ends in self-recovery.

– Fulton J. Sheen

CHAPTER 3
The Colours of Love

The rainbow of love

LOVE IS A RAINBOW

Colours, like features, follow the changes of the emotions.

— Pablo Picasso

It is hard for us, humans, to think of love only in neutral terms of philosophical musings. Our daily life presents us with every colour of feeling and emotion. We are used to associating emotions with colours. For example, yellow feels like joy, "blues" are sadness, we call jealousy "a green-eyed monster", etc. Let us use the same approach as we explore what romantic love feels like.

This seems fitting, because… because, dear Friend, as you have probably experienced yourself, the beginning of love is so different from the end, and in between… have you ever felt so happy, or so angry, or so bitter, or so grateful, or so joyful, or quite so devastated… before you met her?

Everyone we encounter makes us feel some emotions, but our beloved seems to be a source of the most intense fervours, both positive and negative ones. This is inevitable, don't you think? For they are the person we spend most of our time with and have the thinnest protective barrier from.

Dear Friend, what do you think? Does one have to experience the emotions of every colour, including the most debilitating and irksome ones, to attain lifelong, beautiful and passionate romantic love? Is this a requirement of sorts – to taste an entire rainbow?

Or, rather, it is simply inevitable that, whilst sharing life with another person for a long time, you will have been laid bare to an ample sweep of emotional and practical dilemmas.

Finally, whilst it's a lover's delight to penetrate deep inside your essence, he will discover not just the stacks of treasures but also some demons – which might provoke a beast or two within himself. Moreover, the very treasures inside you could evoke a bitter vexation in your lover's soul all the same.

Whichever way you look at it, if your darling has brought out both the best and the worst in you, it's unlikely that you will be looking for somebody else. Both because of the profound contentedness and sheer exhaustion.

The rainbow of romantic love is complex and fluid. With the rainbow in the sky, all the colours are separate from each other, and their sequence is predictable.

It's not the same with love – the possible colour combinations are endless and often occur at the same time, to heighten our confusion. Don't worry, though!

If you become aware of all the colours, analyse them with your mind, understand them with your heart… then the love rainbow becomes your ally, not a foe. Eventually, you might even feel like an expert and could peacefully play it as if it were a piano.

THE COLOUR RED

And yet I have had the weakness, and have still the weakness, to wish you to know with what a sudden mastery you kindled me, heap of ashes that I am, into fire.

– Charles Dickens

The colour we seem to desire the most is red; the colour red is how romantic love always starts. The rainbow starts with the red colour, too! A mere coincidence…?

We associate red with passion; what is passion? Passion is a persuasive and intense love energy. Depending on the intensity, it could feel like a flutter of soft feathers… refreshing twinkling waterfall… or an exploding volcano! We want and enjoy all of them.

THE FORMULA OF PASSION

Between men and women there is no friendship possible. There is passion, enmity, worship, love but no friendship.

— Oscar Wilde

(If you like, you could listen to the following piece of classical music as a soundtrack to the section that follows: Ludwig van Beethoven, Egmont)

Dear Friend, from chapter 1 you will remember that the essence of the universe is a constant movement of love – or energy.

The only way this could be achieved is if the two following conditions are met: first – forms of life do exist; second – the mechanism of polarity is always maintained.

Why? Well, let us think logically. In the universe that is made up of inanimate objects only, the following happens. Physics perspective: energy moves from hot to cold, or from high pressure to low pressure (the polarity principle at work) until equal temperature/pressure is reached throughout the system. This is called equilibrium, when there is no polarity and no movement of energy. Chemistry perspective: chemical reactions, between all entities, might continue for a very long time, but not indefinitely. Once the reactions are completed, the same thing happens – equilibrium, no polarity and no movement of energy.

On the other hand, forms of life are capable of initiating, restarting and modifying the energy flow (as described in "Love: your connection with the universe" in chapter 1). Amongst all forms of life, the most intelligent ones (humans and the like) are the most powerful energy movers.

Humans transport both "physical energy" (altering the landscapes, the atmosphere, sending rockets into space, etc.)

and "emotional energy" (please wait for this to be discussed in detail in "How you connect to the universe" in chapter 4).

OK, so humans are powerful energy movers, but how does the universe make sure that they never, ever stop; in other words, that polarity is always maintained and equilibrium is not reached? Via creating a mechanism which makes equilibrium highly undesirable. Equilibrium, both in metaphysical and the human sense is the absence of movement – the absence of love. And the absence of love hurts us, very much!

This need for polarity is the very reason that romantic love came to exist in the first place. Romantic love is not known in animals other than humans (and, possibly, other intelligent forms of life, currently unknown to us).

There is a natural polarity between a male and female. As already stated above, we feel incomplete without each other, for each of us is a bearer of a different type of energy. We feel a sort of antipathy towards each other; rephrasing that, we are always aware of the danger we pose to each other – danger which losing control might bring. This keeps us at a safe distance – apart from those times when we are close.

N.B. Not to offend any animals, a phenomenon similar to romantic love might exist in some species (for example, swans). But for most animals, the need to procreate and rear young is the only reason for forming a couple; the latter usually ceases to exist once the former is achieved.

So if polarity is always maintained, the energy keeps moving, again and again and again, the cycles are endless, equilibrium is never reached – romantic love never ends, and the universe continues to exist.

But how to maintain the polarity that persists? What does this polarity mean, in a context of human behaviour?

1. PAIN AND PLEASURE

On a level of basic sensations, our behaviour is influenced by two only – those of pleasure and pain. Romantic love is a unique human experience, for it combines both. Dear Friend, please read the following sentence several times. *Pain is the essence of romantic love – please don't complain, and try to learn to enjoy it.* A combination of pain and pleasure feels far more appealing to us than pleasure alone; in other words, if you have experienced suffering, you will appreciate happiness more fully and more acutely than if you never felt the former. As a human is not at liberty not to do what gives him the greatest pleasure, we are "programmed" to prioritise romantic love above anything else in our lives.

Pains of love be sweeter far than all other pleasures are.

– John Dryden

And the two main reasons for pain?

Reason one – an endless uncertainty (loves me, loves me not; do I love her more than she loves me? etc). We are made in such a way that we are attracted to someone who loves us more/or loves us less than we love them. There is no such thing as "equal love" for it would mean polarity is lost. Note that the polarity in romantic love changes, and really quite often.

Love is suffering. One side always loves more.

– Catherine Deneuve

There is scarcely any passion without struggle.

– Albert Camus

Reason two – the most painful distress there is – conflicting emotions. For you can see both beautiful and ugly qualities in your lover; plus, you are aware that whilst he/she is making you feel very happy, it is the very same person who is causing you the most fierce pains.

2. BARENESS AND CONCEALMENT

We yearn to be close and completely open with our loved one; we desire to "become one" with them. The next moment, we are very much aware that some secrets have to be kept. This could be seen as partially caused by modesty (see more below), plus – mystery maintains the excitement. Why is a beautiful female body far more tantalising scantily dressed than fully naked? Because it's a hidden bareness.

Love ceases to be a pleasure when it ceases to be a secret.

– Aphra Behn

I love you as certain dark things are to be loved, in secret, between the shadow and the soul.

– Pablo Neruda

3. MALE AND FEMALE

Maintaining male and female roles is crucial for polarity.

With civilisation came "modesty", where women started to cover private parts of their body, and learned to behave in subtle and retiring ways. This creates mystery, heightens desire and lengthens the duration of courting; all important for establishing and maintaining the intensity of romantic love.

Having different roles helps to maintain mystery and attraction, as well as making us feel contented and happy. What makes a man feel contented and happy is very different to what a woman needs to feel like that; the simplest example being – feeling respected is essential for a man, whilst being adored and desired is what a woman longs for.

Pain is the same thing as pleasure; who loves whom more changes constantly; we want to be open but definitely keep secrets – is there any wonder that poets and writers keep calling love "madness"?

There is always some madness in love. But there is also always some reason in madness.

— Friedrich Nietzsche

When love is not madness it is not love.

— Pedro Calderón de la Barca

Some people claim that love is a "mental illness" precisely because of the characteristics described above.

There can be lunacy without love, but is there any great love without a little lunacy?

— Yochanan Tversky

But love's a malady without a cure.

— John Dryden

But, dear Friend, do you not think that calling love a mental illness is misguided?

Romantic love is the healthiest and the most human of all human experiences. The most healthy because it could promote and maintain every aspect of your health. The most human because humans (plus unknown forms of life) are both capable of romantic love and enabled by it to be the main mover(s) of the universe's energy.

So how do you maintain passion with someone you've been with for years?

Simply remember the formula of passion, and you will succeed.

Don't remove the uncertainty from her mind — she needs it; allow him to feel the pain — he will not admit it, but he wants it.

The value of a woman is proportionate to the amount of suffering she is capable of inflicting upon us.

– Stendhal, *Love*

If you are a male, be masculine; if you are a female, be feminine… and whatever you do, always remain a mystery to your lover.

Dear Friend, I hear your confused cries, I do! Are we supposed to "pain" our lover or heal their wounds (as discussed in "Love is the drug" in chapter 2)?

Well, multitasking the subtleties was never going to be easy… but you might choose to regard your love as the most amazing adventure there is. Plus, you do agree with what William says, don't you?

All the world's a stage, and all the men and women merely players… one man in his time plays many parts.

– William Shakespeare

THE SHADES OF RED

(If you like, you could listen to the following piece of classical music as a soundtrack to the section that follows: Georges Bizet, "Habanera" from Carmen*)*

As intimated above, passion is characterised by different degrees of intensity. Our experiences vary with this regard, and this is not an accident.

We all know, deep inside, what we want/can handle; this could change during our lifetime and is linked to our biological characteristics. To give an example, not every heart could be subjected to a certain degree of stress ("heartbreak") without heart disease ensuing.[3] Individual brains are able to cope with varying degrees of conflicting emotions/trouble, before the health of the former is endangered, etc..

The examples below demonstrate the various shades of passion.

STRAWBERRIES AND CREAM

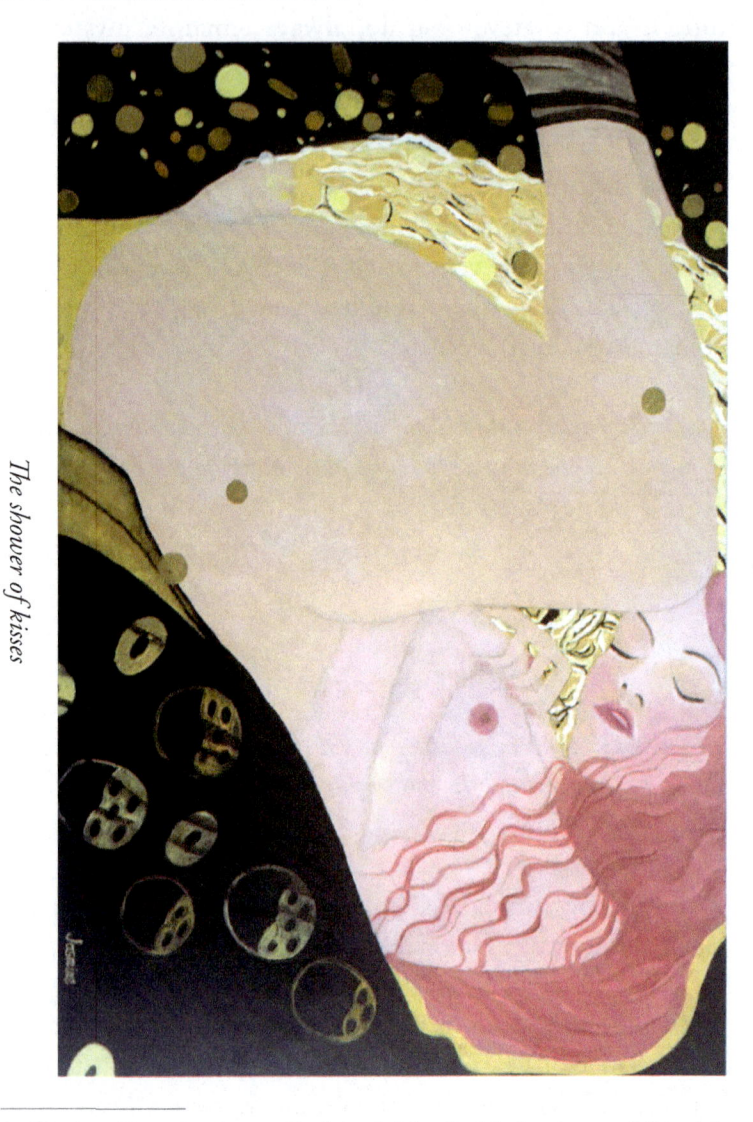

The shower of kisses

---

3. "Broken Heart Syndrome: Evolving Molecular Mechanisms and Principles of Management", Yashendra Sethi, Hamsa Murli et al. J Clin Med, Jan 2023.

ANNIE'S STORY

Your sleeping face on my pillow spreads my lips into the sweetest smile every morning when I awake before you. The morning wash of all-over kisses you dress me with when your eyes open is my very private reason for not needing any morning shower... no showers, it's a fact! Until you are back home at the end of the day, for I will only wash off the traces of your lips when I know there will be more kisses coming soon.

You ask me, really quite often, how is it possible that I love you...? This surprises me and is hard to answer... for I can only know the best in you, you see... It's only you who knows the rest.

And when I say I never wanted to love a man before and was merely allowing myself to be adored... it is your turn to be surprised.

CHERRY LIQUOR

We are all scared to share what is most private and most worrying and most painful and most important; yet we really, really want to.

Love takes off masks that we fear we cannot live without and know we cannot live within.

— James Baldwin

Perversely, we will only reveal those intimate details to someone who makes us feel frightened... for if he doesn't, he could not possibly be the right man.

Don't just undress me, tease me.... scare me a little...

"I've been to Rio, many times, I've met those gorgeous women... yet none of them had touched my heart... what have you done to me...?

You've made me think, I have this hope, I ask myself, oh why? Why is my life always so miserable?

I want, I hope, but never dare...

I need to find the courage and I will.

That little gap between your teeth is the best part, I feel...

You like to dance, we went to a club, your hips are swaying, gorgeous skirt... am at your feet not quite... but still... the other people noticed...

It's the contrast... your innocence and your spellbinding eyes... You do not know your power yet... You knew no passion... my heart says...

but how I wish to be the man to witness that...

... don't break my heart! But if you must, it's better if it's soon... oh baby... I want you so bad...

I'LL ALWAYS WELCOME YOU."

*

"This is not dancing... you are caressing me..." she murmured as his fingers trembled lightly across her back...

They ended up in bed and she honestly could not remember how; she took off her skirt but her white lacy top and black tights were staying on; she made sure of that... and when his lips started her, finding her under the top... *"I cannot handle this... I cannot handle it at all..."* He moved away...

The next thing she remembers is her mouth inside of his... completely encircled by his lips (is this kissing?), and there he kept it, all night, and in the morning – swollen bruised flower of a drunken cherry, where her lips used to be... his body, shaking badly, but controlled...

"You are scaring me!"
"I am sorry, darling… it's just that it's been such a long time…"

You cannot be ready for passion until you are.

EMILY'S STORY

After a few years of marriage, she has gotten used to her husband, especially after they had a child. But there was no passion, no romance – a habit, perhaps? – and a caring sort of pity, that a woman always feels for a man.

She knew she needed more… The dreams, the fire, the awakening even. Such bottomless longing for him – transplanted into her yearning gaze. Her body – restless; the quivering unknown… Oh, what will happen…? When… ? She knew, in her heart, it wouldn't be long… She lay awake most nights.

Who this amazing man will be, she couldn't really tell… her husband? Maybe, she just needs to try and look more pretty; will it help? Red lipstick, cutie heels, bouncy locks… he never seemed to notice.

Warm summer's day… frustrations feel appeased… the dizzy bees are drunk on honey, the scent of roses wrapped around her… a little rest with cup of tea… oh, what bliss…

The sudden blare from the street… her peace deranged… It's a new neighbour moving in.

When he started flirting with her, she felt, with alarm, such a strong pull towards him, his dark and tender eyes, beguiling… She tried to fight it, she really did! In spite herself, she wanted to do the right thing – she's married, after all.

Like a bull, he pursued her without any shadow of a doubt… It was this persistence that filled her with fear… She could sense that he is not scared of him; she felt it in her bones – that he is not going to give up trying...

She filled all his thoughts, day and night; there was no respite from it... inside his mind, he was kissing her, his mouth overflowing with the words of love he did not know he knew.

The leafy trees in her garden, tall dark shadows... they have been touched by her gaze! His hand was stroking them... He did not understand these things before.

By the time the autumn came, he knew... his mind was made up.

Hell-bently, he waited outside, every night. It was raining hard; his numbing fingers warmed by steady breath... for many long weeks... he never missed a night – willing for her to know...

A woman's shadow, all wrapped up, slowly moved towards him... two or three steps... then stopped... It's HER! ... His heartbeat... a strangling cast-iron drum, deep inside his throat... He pulled her towards him, such a supple, yielding body, burning...

Soon, the entire town learned about the affair... The women narrowed their eyes with contempt and envy, and the girls marvelled how proudly she carried her beautiful and nervy head.

They strolled the streets in broad daylight – her eyes resting inside of his; their clumsy, pausing feet saw no one.

The liaison was so mad, so audacious, the flame of their passion so shameless; them not trying to hide, defying all the norms, looking blacker and thinner, every day, right in front of everyone... It humbled people.

Three weeks with no sleep exhausted him; his black stubble took on a shade of blueness... his sunken eyes, dark and dry... deep hollows under her eyes, black as in mourning... Kissing his face, neck, arms with a frenzied abandon, she whispered breathlessly: "Darling! I want to go away; far, far away, let's! I don't care..."

And you cannot stop the passion once it's started.

His love was no longer merely admiration of her beauty, pride in the possession of her. Their joy was thenceforward of a far higher nature, the flame that devoured them was more intense. They underwent transports of utter madness… it assumed at times the aspect of crime.

– Stendhal, *Scarlet and Black*

LIQUORICE, ANYONE?

It is a well-known fact that the physical side of an intimate relationship can turn to extremes – such as violence, derogatory behaviour, bestiality, etc. This is documented, for example, in classic literature:

She would go down on all fours in her chemise on her fur rags, prowling around and growling, as though she wanted to eat him… and he loved this humiliation, relished the pleasure of being an animal… they were maddened by sex, thrown into the delirious imaginations of the flesh… the terrors of their sleepless nights were turning now into a thirst for bestiality…

– Émile Zola, *Nana*

Experimenting with that sort of behaviour, however, doesn't seem to bring us feeling of happiness or contentment, or increase affection for our "partner in crime"; just the opposite in fact.

We seem to start feeling hatred, and even commit an extreme violence, to our lover – the person who had witnessed us degrading our own spirit in that way. (See movies *In the Realm of Senses*, *Bitter Moon*, etc.)

Oh, but real passion, it has no limits, right? And the world of intimacies is endlessly enticing, terrifying, mesmerising, so please, please, DO NOT tell me what to do or not to do with my lover…!

Remember, when I wore those lacy things… with the cut-out bits? I thought they were fun, but you felt uneasy… A minute later, it was my turn to be scared. Your eyes… some wicked green, neonic even, shone through the middle (of the chocolate brown that I love)… if I believed in demons, their eyes would look like that.

What seems to make all the difference is how deeply you fall in love spiritually *before* your daring experiments with the bodily sensations will commence.

> *Your soul is well aware how to lead you into becoming "one flesh". But if you begin with the body… the body knows not where to lead you, except into more and more sensations of the flesh, which by themselves have no power to feed love's deeper hunger.*
>
> – Linda Goodman, *Love Signs*

GRAND PASSION

"Grand passion" is a fascinating subject that has inspired a colossal volume of art and literature over the centuries. Grand passion is also known as "dark passion", quite aptly so – typically, one or both lovers die – like Romeo and Juliet, or Anna and Vronsky, Julien and Madam de Renal, etc., etc.

> *Madam de Renal was faithful to her promise… she did not take her own life, but three days after Julien's death, died…*
>
> – Stendhal, *Scarlet and Black*

Dark love

Curiously, when one lover attempts to kill the other, this spurs on a greater passion in the heart of the surviving victim.

> *He is worthy to be my master, since he has been on the point of killing me... how many men are able to arrive at such an impulse of passion?*

> – Stendhal, *Scarlet and Black*

> *"Will you not love me then?"*
> *"Never..."*
> *"... well, in that case... no one can have you!"*
> *With an unhuman force, Kallist had pushed Beatrice off the cliff... her dress, caught by the boxwood shrub, it saved her from abyss...*
> *"She will hate me now!" Kallist's eyes welled up with despair...*
> *"... quite to the contrary – she will adore you," said Félicité."*
>
> – Honoré de Balzac, *Béatrix*

Dear Friend, why do you think this game of love and death is so irresistible to the human psyche?

When your lover is ready to die for you/attempting to kill you, we feel it shows, beyond doubt, the immensity of love that we have inspired. Furthermore, it confirms that your murderous lover is above the average human being... albeit in a gruesome way.

But romantic love is a life force...! It's full of light, not darkness – I hear you protest. Well, to put it a little coarsely, "Dark passion is a romantic love with no breaks installed."

Romantic love has its cruel moments (out of necessity, as we've learned by now), but it always knows when to stop... you will hurt her just enough, but not too much.

If it's not a murder, how does dark passion kill?

Your love emotions are affecting your brain and your heart (see more in "Mind, body and heart" in chapter 4). The size of the latter, the number of associated nerve fibres, the levels of chemical substances that run through them are determined by biological characteristics of the human; their functional capacity is, therefore, *not infinite*. Too much impact in a way of stressors and we die; from heart attack or from brain haemorrhage and similar related conditions... or from taking our own life.

Those of us who are more in tune with our bodies, and more in control of our emotions, are able to both perceive what level of stress we can handle without endangering our survival and alter our behaviour accordingly. People with less ability to understand and control themselves are more vulnerable as a result.

In case you are rejoicing in being one of those "strong and controlled people", please consider being humble – and thoughtful. You might meet someone who will have such a profound impact on you that you will no longer be sure of your own nature. It is also possible that you will have such a devastating effect on someone else that their vulnerabilities will not be able to stand it.

One must not trifle with love.

– Alfred de Musset

Dear Friend, most of us will not die from dark passion, but don't you think there are snippets of it in our daily lives?

Bitter Vine
A POEM

I gave you bitter vine of love, all night!
you did not know…
And in the morning – gloomy eyes… a long drive to your
*   work…*
Am feeling guilty – just a drop, and worried – little bit.
For… don't you know…? In the novels
They kill their male characters
Galloping their horses
Heads full of love's doubts…

My vine is bitter

RENALDO'S STORY

Your perfect grace, it gleams me up... your kisses... no other woman has such lips.

You frighten me... I cannot trust a word you say... I cannot stay away!...

You used to tell me I am ugly, and you just love me for my soul... so you don't love me anymore? What...? You "can explain"...? Whatever do you mean? No, please don't say a word!

I'm maddened by despair... wild, dirty dog is what I am... your little heel, bear me down... those shoes? HOW MUCH? Yes, you can have them...

Dear Friend, do you agree with Ferdinand's observation?

> *The most powerful weapon on earth is the human soul on fire.*
>
> – Ferdinand Foch

Just like a fire, love should be handled with care… as much as humanly possible, that is. The comparison with fire seems apt, for the power of love can bring about miracles, or cause destruction and death.

THE COLOUR ORANGE

> *Human love has little regard for the truth. It makes the truth relative, since nothing, not even the truth, must come between it and the beloved person.*
>
> – Dietrich Bonhoeffer

(If you like, you could listen to the following piece of classical music as a soundtrack to the section that follows: Erich W. Korngold, "Cello Concerto in C Major")

Just like in a rainbow, the colour red is blended with the colour orange.

The "trickery", the artfulness are an important part of love and not some troublesome nuisance; it is a necessity. Perhaps we could discuss why?

THE PREY AND A HUNTER

"Who was the prey; who was a hunter? It's all so devilishly upside down," as a popular song goes.

ANTONIA'S STORY

He gave her a tall red rose and a letter. She was surprised; opened it – a love declaration! And she barely even noticed him before – just one of the men at work.

It was flattering of course, but she felt nothing. She said kind words; he cried.

He moved away and started writing to her. She answered – it's rude not to, and plus – it's fun! What happens if I write this…? Or respond like that…?

It never ceased to amaze her just how easy it was. Look that way, say these words… very soon – he is done for. How on earth does one go about choosing the right man if they are ALL, hmm… "susceptible"? But there is a catch – as you push him into the deep waters, more likely than not, you'll get dragged in, too – unless, that is, you are "a professional" [see "The colour black" later in this chapter]… By the seventh letter, she loved him a little.

Dear Friend, it is perhaps true that a woman can *attract* any man, but she cannot know which one is *capable of loving her the best*; therefore, he must, and does, self-select.

A man is the one who leads the love story. A woman cannot do it, and she does not want to.

Deep inside, she longs to be "your baby" (anytime she feels like it, that is). How can she do it if you are not in control?

No matter how much you adore her, you can't relax – you are in charge.

– Michael Weller, *The Hunter of the Hearts*

Among thousands of happy couples that I've seen over decades, their behavioural pattern was ALWAYS like that. Could this be the only thing that works…?

Without the artfulness in romantic love, the mystery, fear and uncertainty all disappear – and yet they are all absolutely necessary for passion to appear and to endure (as detailed in "The tragedy of romantic love" and "The formula of passion" in chapter 2).

In small ways, we all know what needs to be done, but some people seem to be much more skilled in the art of love.

The French are widely regarded as a nation of great lovers. Is there some historical truth in that?

French classic authors have plentifully documented how widespread the artfulness of love is in their society. For example, "pique", or a stirring of one's vanity, seems to be a tool that is routinely used in order to make someone fall in love with you. If you show attention to the sister you favour less, it is almost guaranteed that the other sister will feel curious and envious. Taking on a mistress for a few months after marriage in order to hurt your young wife's feelings will be enough to make her feel attached to you deeply, etc. According to Stendhal, these sorts of behaviours were practised as a matter of routine by entire layers of the society.

And what about the modern France? There seems to be a great tolerance, acceptance even, of spouses having extramarital liaisons. For as long as the latter are kept "respectable", they are deemed to promote the stability of long marriage.

Husbands frequently make sure of the love of their wives for many long years by taking a little mistress two months after marriage.

– Stendhal, *Love*

Desire, in this confident but still virginal nature, has been whipped up by the astute tactics of Nana, resulting in terrible ravages in the long run… This solemn gentleman bit his pillow at night and sobbed in frustration as the same sensual images floated into his head.

– Émile Zola, *Nana*

The effort that he was imposing on himself to appear cured in the eyes of Mathilde absorbed all his spiritual strength: "I ought not even to allow myself to press to my heart this supple and charming form, or she will despise and abuse me. What a frightful nature!"

– Stendhal, *Scarlet and Black*

Yes, I will marry her; but this doesn't mean anything needs to change between us, my darling!

– Guy de Maupassant, *Bel-Ami*

Whether we like it or not, this is how it works with us humans. We crave mystery and excitement that give us just the right degree of emotional turbulence… We will hold on to a skilled lover who can create it for us.

THE COLOUR YELLOW

The deeper that sorrow carves into your being, the more joy you can contain. When you are joyous, look deep into your heart and you shall find it is only that which has given you sorrow that is giving you joy.

– Kahlil Gibran

(If you like, you could listen to the following piece of classical music as a soundtrack to the section that follows: Pyotr Ilyich Tchaikovsky, "Dance of the Sugar Plum Fairy" from The Nutcracker*)*

Yellow is a colour of happiness, joy and sunshine. How often is romantic love like that? Just as the rays of sunshine are interspersed by foggy skies expectant with rains, the sharp needles of acute joy and rolling giggles in your head are separated by moody days and tumultuous nights.

―――

LIZZY AND JAMES'S STORY

Seeing you always makes me smile inside, your serious face is endlessly fascinating because… because you are puzzled, earnestly, deeply! by what is extremely easy for me, and yet you effortlessly handle the stresses that make me hide in the corner and cry. You are the source of an endless enigma and deep warm twinkling inside me.

It's a sunny day at the beach. You spread your towel under me, and as I gaze at the waves – they lick the pebbles, audacious… my mind drifts away; it's in a dream… Suddenly, I am startled! Your hand lies on my back… motionless first; then moving slowly… like, for five minutes! Am feeling charmed but shocked… those other people on the beach, embarrassed eyes averted… it's new, raw love (only a third date), and they can feel it…

The breeze is fresh, and your hands (the shape looks right – it's so important)… moved your jacket onto my shoulders… They feel so gentle, plus that reckless back massage… Will you be a passionate lover? I hope so, because otherwise – I couldn't…

The crunchy sand under my foot, am fluttering my toes… I see you've noticed, shy, jumping eyes…

Oh, but it is SO SUNNY! I smile and laugh, and you take lots of photos. You'll frame one of them, and on your desk that sunny day becomes eternal.

*

When she said "yes", agreed to that third date... a tiny word... I had two sleepless nights...

You feel like a fairy... so ethereal... you could just disappear and it nightmares me...

How can I lose you now! Just as I've found you... so many years. I can't believe we've met...

I chose the beach, the seas are where my spirit lives... I feel at home... as ease when I am here...

At ease...? Your tiny foot, how could I BREATHE...? When you just moved it... miracle, indeed... I did not know what else to do... The spasms of joy, of pain, my voice gives in... It's hard to speak, you're quiet, thanks to heavens... My hand drops onto you... I melt... I die... My little darling, you don't know it yet – but YOU ARE MINE.

She makes me laugh... Who else could say those things? Her words this morning:

How is that even possible that you feel like a tonne... resting on top of me... and then melt into nothingness when you roll me on my side and our legs entwine? You've changed the law of physics...! Only took you two seconds.

Dear Friend, yellow might not be the most prevalent colour of the rainbow... but even when you are feeling blue, please remember Oscar's words:

A flower blossoms for its own joy.

– Oscar Wilde

Whatever else is happening in your life, and whichever the phase of your romantic love, please never forget to keep blossoming.

THE COLOUR GREEN

Jealousy is that pain which a man feels from the apprehension that he is not equally beloved by the person whom he entirely loves.

— Joseph Addison

(If you like, you could listen to the following piece of classical music as a soundtrack to the section that follows: Gustav Mahler – Symphony No. 4, second movement)

Dear Friend, we commonly associate the colour green with jealousy. But did you know that many lovers experience an equally troublesome emotion of envy? Both shades of green feel highly unpleasant – green is one of the most taxing colours of love's rainbow.

ILONA'S STORY

I got to know all your beautiful qualities, and I am not envious – not a drop. I get to be proud of you and benefit from all the goodness of your character. You got to know my appealing traits and are, oftentimes, envious of them... Why, or why? It feels so wrong – why can't you feel a part of me so all I have is yours, also? You will feel that... you have to hurt yourself and me first, though – until this hurdle is passed, too.

Italian philosopher and writer Dante Alighieri, in his *Divine Comedy*, describes a story of Madonna Pia, a very beautiful noble lady who was also the sole heiress of the richest family in Sienna. She was faithful to her husband, but her multiple advantages made him feel so envious of her that he planned and executed her ruthless murder.

Many Russian writers describe the centuries-long tradition amongst uneducated masses where husbands have a weekly ritual of getting deeply drunk and then battering their wives into immobility, for no other reason than to get their frustration with them out of their system.

Please note how telling this is: without the harness of education, and with disinhibition caused by drink, humans act on pure instinct.

Greek philosophers, as always, see right through it:

Once made equal to man, woman becomes his superior.

— Socrates

Dear Friend, from the examples above, do you see the pattern?

For love to be harmonious, a woman should be a muse for her man, not a competition that hurts his ego.

OK, great! Embracing one's femininity helps to safeguard your love from envy, but what about jealousy? Is it avoidable?

Some people say jealousy is not part of love… "it's only insecure people that are jealous".

Do you agree with this statement? Possibly — "yes" and "no". If she is so secure in your love (how unwise are you…), she might ignore the *unconfirmed suspicions*. But if the suspicions are confirmed, and she is still not jealous… well, then she either ceased loving you entirely, or her love has reached the highest highs.

True love has its sophisticated weaknesses… you can see that you are being cheated on and yet pretend not to notice.

— Honoré de Balzac, *Béatrix*

Dear Friend, the sentiment described by Honoré, albeit arguably admirable, is not pertinent to many; most of us struggle with forgiving an unfaithful lover and some of us choose to move on.

Many women have this ability to tear love out of their hearts – completely. They make sure they never see their previous lover – literally, never again – and teach their heart to forget him entirely. "Who is he? Never existed – all gone."

Are those women wicked and cruel…? Or just the opposite – very tenderly sensitive? For just a single, tiny memory of him would entirely destroy her ability to… brush her hair… go shopping… not to cry all day long… just a survival instinct.

A Drink of Flowers
A POEM

Am drinking flowers all day… it makes my mood just right…
I will not think, I will, I won't!
Where have you been all night?
I'll go away, I'll find myself, again!
I'll be all new…
I know I can… I plan… I will… I will stop loving you.

Dear Friend, the example above implied a lovesick female, but of course, all of us could suffer that way. If you don't manage to save yourself via negating the passion, you could meet a tragic end.

Jealousy is bred in doubts. When those doubts change into certainties, then the passion either ceases or turns to absolute madness.

– François de La Rochefoucauld

JANELLE'S STORY

She knew he loved someone before he married her… well, most men did… it wouldn't matter – she felt sure.

The spring! It came… the daffodils, warm rains… Time for a new start, he thought.

Her eyes, so brave and blue… smile timorous, reserved; two tiny stones – the girlish breasts; he planned to love her… She said yes…

It took him a few weeks to feel, with fear, with the inwards rage, that she, the first one…! stuck in his heart – is like a pin; a pin that hooked… and every time that his heart moves is piercing him deeper…

New wife… so shy, so cold? She is not feeling him…

The other one! Her passion frenzied, the molten heat, she drew all night…

They met again, just in the shop; it was not planned.

Her smudgy stains of restless eyes, evasive smile…

"How is your life with your new wife?"

"Oh well, you know!" is all he said, hastening away… (escape her loving gaze!)… He went straight home, forgot the milk…

It took a while… backwards and forwards; it's hurting him, it's hurting them; the married home – he left one day…

The dusty winds, that summer was so hot… tried to be kind… he knew she is not well – was told she's all greyed up… He never went to that, to her part of town… could do no more for her.

The window opened by itself (must be the draught?), the sand on her teeth, it's hard to breathe…

"Just tidying my cupboards"… silk top, pale blue, the one she wore the day they met…

… all shaken with the sudden sobs.

Her mother noticed. "What is wrong?"

Her lips dry, cold; the pallor almost ashen; the wobbly legs… She managed wooden smile:

"I am OK…"

"I'm worried about you... Why don't you see a doctor?"

With sudden anger, the scream that wanted out, she couldn't stifle anymore: "Well, stop your worrying then!!!"

A few days later, when her girlfriends came, she felt a little better... life goes on...? agreed she'll go with them...

A balmy night lit up the beer garden, the reckless crickets chirping for females...

Her bubbly girlfriends giggling...

Trying to laugh, trying to smile, she must hide her tortured pining.... the other one, victorious, the gorgeous... no thinking, STOP!

Then... people laugh! Insulting her; mudlarks to her pain... "A two-faced whore! She cheated with old man; that's why her husband left her" – bloodthirsty teenagers' loud scorn.

Discomfit, mortified... her soul, brim-full of pain and shame; her burning cheeks – awash with sudden tears... she left the party... curiously – felt glad... decision formed; well – it's the end.

She flees the prurient eyes...

The hurried run, on swaying, drunk-like legs... she's biting bleeding lips... Back home straight to the kitchen; knife, the cooling blade, it calms her...

Gathered all her strength... wild burning sting, the carrot crunching sound...

Knife in her chest... the heaving wave of blinding pain, the needles in her ears...

She feels no more.

Whatever the shade of green we experience towards our loved one – envy or jealousy or both – those are challenging times. You might be lucky to acquaint yourself with only a drop of each that vanishes from your soul very fast... well, once the universe is satisfied you've had the awareness of them in any case.

THE COLOUR BLUE

The word "happy" would lose its meaning if it were not balanced by sadness.

— Carl Jung

(If you like, you could listen to the following piece of classical music as a soundtrack to the section that follows: John Williams, "Theme from Schindler's List*")*

Dear Friend, the blues, the sadness… such a beautiful colour of love, do you agree? If there needs to be a contrast – and there is – then gentle moodiness… a touch of sorrow, a little cry… offsets the passion, gives us resting time. Some shades of blue are darker than others.

Loving the blues

"Why does he never kiss my toes… (well, he does, but only if I've stubbed one, and it hurts)? They are very pretty! Of that I am sure…"

"Hmm, I don't know, but does it REALLY matter?" my friend despairs. "I bet he kisses everything else."

"Oh, but it SO does! Don't you know that love is 'talking to every little toe, separately'."

"Sometimes I am not sure how you feel. At other times I feel that you don't love me… or love me but not enough… or not the way I need to be loved… This does make me feel so sad and so very, very blue. Or slightly blue – it just depends on the situation. And one day you said that you don't love me. Then you took those words back – later, the same day. Those dark days… you were so confused about what love actually is, you felt so puzzled, and you even told me so. Those days are long gone, because I have since learned that love has many colours, and it's only the colour black that is the absence of love."

*

"I don't feel happy… not been for a while; I don't know why; could this be you…? If so, it's easy! I'll just go… I went… It felt no better… this crazy fever shaking me… get angry, but don't cry… stagnation… I can't bear it… Do something! Or I'll die…

"Inside my soul… within my heart… it hurts… it's all I really know… My restlessness – how to heal that? I never, nowhere feel at home… The peachy fluff along your neck… the pillow scented with your hair… are in my heart… but they don't help… You just can't understand this…

"I don't love love… it always comes… it's she, then her… It does feel nice…

"but makes no difference…

"Am I a colander… with holes that are just too large?

"My running lips… you know… you don't… are searching… Will you guess what for?

"You are my hope… I crawl in throbs… to reach it… please…! I don't know what."

———

Blues could be a temporary sadness, or they could be profound if one feels that love is ending… This is when the colour blue turns into the colour purple.

THE COLOUR PURPLE

Man is sometimes extraordinarily, passionately in love with suffering, and that is a fact.

– Fyodor Dostoevsky

(If you like, you could listen to the following piece of classical music as a soundtrack to the section that follows: Edvard Grieg, "The Death of Åse (B minor)" from Peer Gynt*)*

Dear Friend, we all fall out sometimes. Some people do it more often than others; sometimes it gets BAD.

———

PETER AND MARY'S STORY

Yes, I am angry…! What are you gonna do about it? "My eyes look terrible?"

Do you think I don't know it? I FEEL it – drowning in my own bile… bitter taste in my mouth… large red vine – every night now.

What happened to you…? Your waist is gone, and so is your sweetness… but at night… when I don't see you – I see you… again…

My brain is cracking up! It's morning, great! I'll go to work, eight hours of peace.

("Bye, sweetheart," say my lips, and touch your nose.)

That girl in the office… OH! Her eyes… so dark and dizzy… are making love to mine, caressing…

If you could only disappear! Can I make you disappear? But what about the kids…?

Am fighting dark thoughts, all the way to work.

*

I am hurting so much, but it feels better to have this pain in my life rather than my life without you.

Your every good quality is known to me, and so is every negative one – this seems to mean it is possible to feel love and dislike all at the same time… in any case, the feelings fluctuate, and often change from one extreme to another – almost instantly. Surely you cannot just stop loving a person if you both hate them and adore them within the very same day… same hour even! … This just makes no sense.

Why is it so hard to give up on you, the source of my suffering? Is it because one hopes that the beautiful love we've shared can come back again, or because after you've known another person that deeply, it feels terribly wasteful somehow to let them go.

And strangely, feeling the pain side of love feels like we have gotten closer, because at times… you show me the glimpses inside the deep of your soul… flushes of light into your darker parts – the sneaky squint of inner eye… cocktail of bravery and not… the "I am always-rightness" but… they are so intimate and inner that it feels – perversely somehow – precious to see you with the mask dropped, just for an instant.

And also… because we are both in pain… and the pain is

caused by love… it is the same thing as being inside the same love… inside – not out…?

I feel so cross…! You dared to stop loving me… Can one respect a man who broke his promises…? And at the same time, your single passing gaze gives me hope… a guarantee even… that all will be healed with the extremes of tenderness that have never even been known to exist before.

I want to shout to you, make you see…! that I have learned to love you deeply, badnesses and all, and that is the best love there is so, surely, you should be at my feet, delighted and grateful? But this not how love works… Only by hurting you can I bring you back, and hurting you is so hard… now that I finally fully love you.

KILLING ME SOFTLY

We know that hurting works. You don't appreciate something you have unless you see that you are close to losing it.

> *You have to make her suffer – always have her mind occupied with the great uncertainty – does he love me? If you don't make her suffer, you will lose her.*
>
> – Stendhal, *Scarlet and Black*

Purple meets orange

The artfulness thus carried out by someone who loves you might well feel cruel, and it is blighting you, but is it really a bad thing, if the sole aim of your lover is to keep passion alive? This is just the orange colour in the spectrum of love… and everyone knows that orange and purple are good together.

CHLOE AND JULIAN'S STORY

Sinking into the office chair, his shoulders crumpled in, as he took his head in his hands: "I don't even know where she is…!"

In the vacuum of his brain, the memories flooded in… later, at night, a sickening image rose constantly in front of his eyes… He tore at the sheets with his teeth, crying and cursing…

*

"Why did you come into my life…? A satisfaction of my whim…? Response to my soul's cry? Your eyes are wrapping me in gauze. I'll try and not succumb… am gazing out of this world; my body, in sweet slumber, betrays befuddled mind."

As she boarded the night-time express, steamy head, her thoughts were doubling; no, they were parallel; this describes it better.

She loved him and missed him; her heart knew it was true. But every time she looked at him, all she wanted to do is cry…

Whilst when she sees the face of the other, she feels a happy laugh… it's an instant reaction… and yet she barely knows him… He is terrifying, which is good, and unavailable, which is bad… or better…? Or doesn't matter?

Soothed by the rhythmic sound of a moving train, she fell asleep… It was a strange dream. Clouded, moist night-time skies… and inside, she is walking – upside down… This made her dizzy, and she started to fall… He caught her…! Not with his arms… with his lips… a few rose petals in between… sweet, sweet pleasure…

When she returned home, he sensed that she is, probably, lying… that he can never fully believe her… but the silky warmth of her cheek on his chest made him feel utterly helpless.

No longer bitter or angry, his exhausted heart had no room for suspicion… he did not want to know. She was back in his arms, and this was all that mattered.

UNBEARABLE

What is hell? I maintain that it is the suffering of being unable to love.

– Fyodor Dostoevsky

(If you like, you could listen to the following piece of classical music as a soundtrack to the section that follows: Carl Orff, Carmina Burana*)*

Dear Friend, emotional pain is part of life, and we get used to feeling it and coping with it.

Emotional pain caused by the one you love is in a class of its own for the distress that follows is the greatest. Conflicting emotions (as already discussed in previous sections) are the hardest ones for our psyche to process.

He's hurt you so many times; you've cried an ocean of tears and after hundreds of hours of thinking, trying to understand, forgive, forget…! making plans… you are still not sure what to do…

And then something happens, and you feel that you simply cannot hold on a minute more. His voice – so cold – his expression – so coarse – his words – so unfeeling and ruthless…! It simply has been the last drop. The first stage, you feel turned into a stone and cannot breathe or move; if you are lucky, this only lasts seconds and you'll start screaming/crying/over breathing – your body fights to return to life.

The worst-case scenario, your brain (your heart?) are exploding in such an agony that this needs to be stopped NOW. You reach out for a handful of pills, a razor, a bottle of acid… you attempt ending your life.

"Ismiidaamin"[4] by Nashira Karasu

I was a medical student when I saw Annette on an ENT ward, and I will never forget her. Only sixteen, transparently slender, she couldn't speak due to the tracheostomy tube in her neck. Her eyes were suffused with such a beautiful naked pain that it felt indecent to look.

Anna Karenina's suicide, and how she came to it, is described

---

4. Translation from Somali: "to seek help" but also "suicide".

in one of the world's greatest eponymous novels by Leo Tolstoy. The circumstances were against Anna – her husband wouldn't give her a divorce, society had ostracised her and she had very little access to her son. But it's the dynamic with her lover, Count Vronsky, that is so poignant... It's not his fault, and it's not her fault, but they are hurting each other's feelings constantly, and what started as a gorgeous romance ends up as an utter misery... He feels his life has ended, too, after she takes hers, and so he goes to war, to die.

> ... *Cold and angry gaze of a person, enraged by being chased and repeatedly threatened, shone in his eyes, whilst his lips were saying tender words to her... She saw this gaze and understood exactly what it meant...*
>
> *In the pangs of jealousy, she reproached him and was looking for new reasons for her reproach, in everything. All that was difficult in her predicament, she was blaming it on him... and everything that she feared that he might do in future, she kept him accountable for, as if he had already done it...*
>
> *... Anna, sweetheart, just tell me, what do you need me to do. I will do anything, ANYTHING...! to make you happy... said he, touched by the immensity of her desperation... anything to avoid you being as miserable as you are now...*
>
> *... it's OK, OK... she said... I don't know myself... it's my loneliness, my nerves... anyway, let's change the subject... She was trying to hide her joy at having won over him, once more...*
>
> – Leo Tolstoy, *Anna Karenina*

Emotions spiralling out of control; overthinking; losing the sense of reality are parts of "passion's anatomy" that Anna and Vronsky demonstrate. If they knew how the human psyche works beforehand, would it have helped them to prevent their tragedy?

Perhaps it would – for love can and does recover; the only condition it behests is that you do not lose your faith in it. But you can't even think straight when your inner agony is immense; never mind feeling faith in your love.

Dear Friend, if your emotions are soaring in an ungovernable fashion, please recognise it, and make yourself and/or your lover safe and away from each other. Nothing positive will happen until you both mellow a little, whilst a spell of separation might well help to avoid love-related suicide/murder, and even rekindle your passion.

It's amazing how someone can break your heart, and you can still love them with all the little pieces.

– Ella Harper

The colour purple often is the end of love, but it does not need to be.

Those people who are patient with their love have learned the secret: there is more than one rainbow! And as we live through different rainbows, over the years, a miracle happens – the worst colours, the purples and the greens… they just disappear.

THE COLOUR BLACK

The man in black travels with your soul in his pocket.

– Stephen King

(If you like, you could listen to the following piece of classical music as a soundtrack to the section that follows: Camille Saint-Saëns, Danse macabre)

Scientifically, colour is an expression of light.

When no light is reflected, you see black.

There is no colour black in the rainbow.

When someone is playing upon your nature with all the calm of a skilled pianist touching the keys, making you fall for them whilst they don't have any love for you in their heart, what is it?

Have you ever wondered about the famous courtesans, the historical femme fatale? Their power was immense – many a man threw their fortunes at their feet and even lost their lives. The wars have started at their whim… dynasties destroyed! Millions of innocent people died, cannon fodder to those wars…

Fairy tales, from every culture, echo those historical truths. The temptresses of folktales made men forget their deeds and journeys, and "inspired them" to murder their own family members, agonising in the madness of jealousy…

Those women… such a power… how did they do it?

Having no regard whatsoever for a man… being armed with an attitude of profound indifference blended with contempt for him… makes a courtesan a mountain that seems perfectly within his reach, yet impossible to climb.

Dear Friend, see – again – a polarity principle at work. "Love for sale" – yet no one can reach her heart … "but maybe I can…?" – a challenge that seems irresistible for some men. The genuine uncaring of a courtesan is an impenetrable shield she paid for dearly, though. Immeasurable suffering/abuse in her early life is the usual cause for the courtesan's soul to become so hardened.

> *… Desire… that she had created, had grown ever stronger and now filled the whole theatre. Now her least gesture breathed longing into them… shoulders leaned forward, muscles vibrated… the backs of their necks tingled…*
>
> *… he felt her taking possession of him, he would have denied everything, sold everything, just to have her for one hour that evening…*

... but how could he ever forget while his brother was still around... his brother replaced him in her bed... his own flesh and blood, whose pleasure made him mad with jealousy. It was the end, he wanted to die.

– Émile Zola, *Nana*

Having achieved infamousness and immense riches, she tends to, almost always, have a bitter end of a lonely death and her wrinkled, dead-eyed face is akin to harrowing black paintings of Goja.

It's not always a woman who is a ruthless charmer. For example, French aristocracy's use of "professional seducers" in order to bring back a wayward spouse/carry out complex family and political intrigues is well documented throughout classic literature.

Here are twenty thousand francs. You need to dazzle and seduce the marquise, make her fall head over heels in love with you... you've got ten days," said the old adventurist.

"If she was a courtesan, this would be impossible; but with an intelligent society woman, it's a done deal," answered him the young adventurist.

– Honoré de Balzac, *Béatrix*

Dear Friend, do you think it's quite likely that the "powerful – paid for – love" phenomenon exists in a modern world, too? Where professional seducers are sought out by people who are thinking differently and want to make things happen, we humans are forever searching for effective ways to influence each other.

Curiously, male adventurists tend to settle down one day, start a family, lead a "normal life", which most female courtesans never, ever achieve.

Perhaps we can conclude that the human psyche is damaged deeply by practicing "love for sale", but women seem to be affected more.

THE COLOUR WHITE

The love we have in our youth is superficial compared to the love that an old man has for his old wife.

— Will Durant

(If you like, you could listen to the following piece of classical music as a soundtrack to the section that follows: Sebastian Bach, "Air on the G String")

Dear Friend, so we have talked about all the colours of love, and "no colour" black; what does the colour white mean?

White heart

MRS SMITH AND MR CLARKSON'S STORIES

One is often downhearted having witnessed an unhappy couple, but to discern the dispirited elderly – that feels downright eerie. It's Valentine Day at work, and I've been chatting to some senior patients this morning.

"Will you and your husband be celebrating, Mrs Smith?"

"We have been married for a long time, Doctor…!" She lifts the weighty eyes at me, her stare sharp and squeezed-out dry… the acquiesced wretchedness personified.

*

"Are you doing something special tonight, Mr Clarkson?"

"It's Valentine Day every day now." He smiles gently, gazing downwards.

Those couples who have been together for decades, grew old together and are still so obviously in love… they are quite rare, but they most certainly do exist; we have all seen them. The aforesaid mellow men and women, do they really spend their days devising and carrying out some complex emotional manipulations of one another, in amongst caring for their grandchildren, so to speak…? Apparently not. There comes a time when you no longer need to do that. It happens when your love has reached its "white colour".

> *If your beloved gives way to her passion and commits the cardinal sin of removing your fear by the intensity of her response, then love loses in intensity (in its fears, that is), but it makes up for it by the charm of complete abandon and infinite trust, becoming a gentle habit which softens the hardships of life and gives a new interest to its enjoyment.*
>
> *– Stendhal,* Love

OK, but how do we get there? If you wanted to be a couple like that, what are you to do?

> *Why is lasting, mutual love so elusive? To reach a complete and permanent union with the other half, man and woman must learn the lessons of twelve sun signs. They must master the wisdom of those twelve mysteries of love before they could achieve a final, perfect harmony between their mental, physical, emotional and spiritual natures.*
>
> — Linda Goodman, *Love Signs*

Linda uses the term "twelve mysteries of love" when she describes human qualities one must learn to harness within oneself, to find a middle point between the extremes — in order to perfect one's nature. For example, patience is good, but the undesirable extreme is stubbornness; devotion is admirable, but the negative side is possessiveness; passion is great, but only if combined with its opposite of surrender, etc.

The colour white is what you get when all the other colours are combined. The red and the orange, the yellow and green, the blues and the purples — all come together to create sunlight, and the rainbow, and an everlasting love.

Dear Friend, if you've lived with your lover through all the colours of the rainbow, your union will have become unbreakable.

CHAPTER 4

In Love with the Universe

Someday, after mastering the winds, the waves, the tides and gravity, we shall harness for God the energies of love, and then, for a second time in the history of the world, man will have discovered fire.

– Pierre Teilhard de Chardin

HOW YOU CONNECT TO THE UNIVERSE

TRANSCENDENCE

The extent of your consciousness is only limited by your ability to love, and to embrace with your love the space around you and all it contains.

– Napoleon Bonaparte

Dear Friend, see the poignant words of Napoleon above; was he being philosophical? Who knows... but they also seem to describe the phenomenon of transcendence, quite literally. When we are in love, our consciousness is able to absorb the energy waves and the information they contain from the space all around us.

You are putting your fingers on my thigh, the outer part, in the little dent between the gym-shaped muscles. Then all you do is slide them up and down a couple of inches, again… and again… (why does it never feel like that when I touch myself…?)… A few minutes later, my entire body is paralysed (did you know that this feels amazing…?) and my consciousness is filled with the large stains of beautiful deep purple… They are all moving and moulding into each other… At other times, it's pale blue or a turquoise. But never emerald… "I want to see the emerald…! Please can you add this to your list…?" I breathe softly in your ear; it's pitch-black, but I am sure I can see your smiling beard.

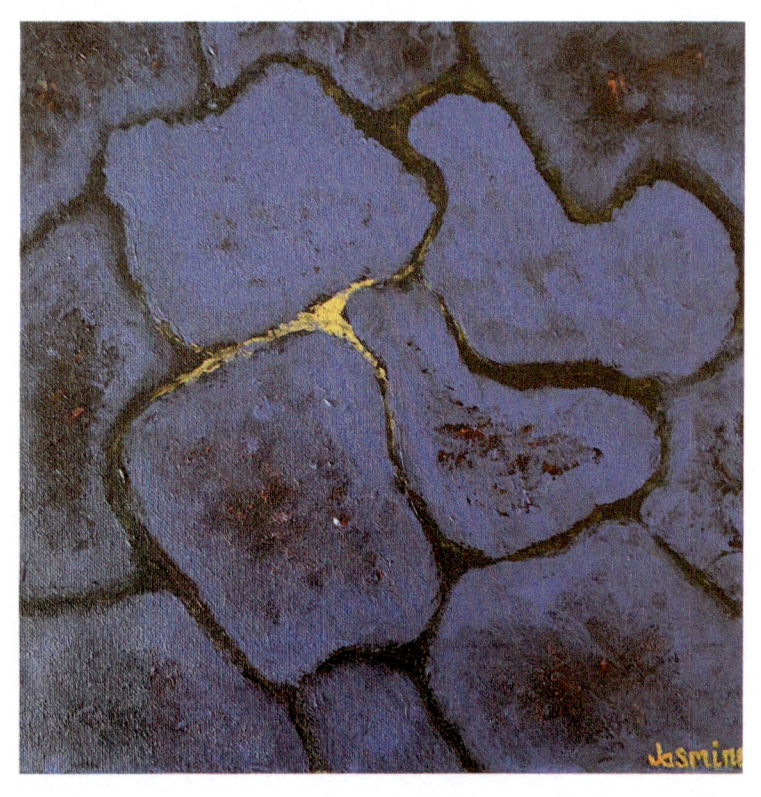

Paint my mind

You are the owner of my thoughts; you live inside my head. I'm trying not to show it, always; my feelings and my fears – shielded. How can I let you in…? I can't. If I'm exposed – you'll think me weak… You'll love me less – this risk, I cannot take! Your soul's little fingertips, will they be gentle? Or will they dig right in, the nervous grace of a wildish cat…? I would forgive you instantly, of course… My love, my pain, the torture of my flesh.

My sharpest inner chord, the maleness in me – the one I guard the most – but you just know; how can you…?

Your every little gesture, passing word – they strike it; pull it in… your touch… hangs my insides on a stabbing hook. I'm rolling upside down… I run from you – I must! I can't… and every night, I ask myself: is this too much – or not enough?

Dear Friend, it's each and every soul's greatest desire to become "one" with the universe *in the moment*; to attain the awareness of the blended consciousness. It is also each soul's greatest desire to find and carry out its unique mission. This process is often *lifelong*.

The second desire links you to all humans, for once all unique missions are accomplished, the tapestry of the universe becomes complete, and we all become "one".

OK, so the second desire is quite a tangible notion, and we have already signposted in the previous sections as to what one needs to do.

What about the first desire? How do you get to feel like one being with the universe, in the moment? Some Eastern leaders advocate breaking all bonds with family and friends, giving up possessions and living in the midst of wilderness, in a shroud of solitude and austerity – for decades! Even then, success is not guaranteed. Others, predominantly Western voices, are offering their expertise on how mind-altering, potentially toxic and even deadly drugs, are the way to go, apparently. The majority of us are unable/unwilling to give up our personal and societal responsibilities/endanger our health for the sake of an individual spiritual indulgence. Is there another way?

In fact, there MUST BE another way. Think about it; if the universe's design implies that it is the greatest desire of the souls to blend with it, the former must have provided some feasible means for achieving the latter, for all of us. Feasible in a sense that we are not required to demolish our normal life routine or accept fatal risks.

Dear Friend, do you think it's possible that the phenomenon of transcendence is an answer? Let us analyse this thoroughly.

Firstly – how does this transcendence come about? We will start with some school-level physics.

The sun's energy is a type of electromagnetic radiation and is a source of energy for everything in the solar system, including humans, other forms of life and all inanimate objects.

In turn, humans, other forms of life and all inanimate objects emit electromagnetic radiation back into the space around them.

Waves interact with each other as they move through space. Depending on the medium they are passing through, they could reflect, retract or bounce back, or continue straight ahead. Notwithstanding the shape of their trajectory, the essence of them being a connecting force between all entities is represented in figure 7. See it again on the opposite page.

Electromagnetic energy emitted by the human body is related to the body's heat; it is called thermal radiation. Thermal radiation is electromagnetic radiation emitted from all matter that is at a non-zero temperature; it includes part of ultraviolet (UV) radiation and all visible and infrared (IR) radiation. Thermal radiation forms an essence of interactions between inanimate entities and the rest of the universe.

Thermal radiation emitted by the human body is mostly in the infrared region.

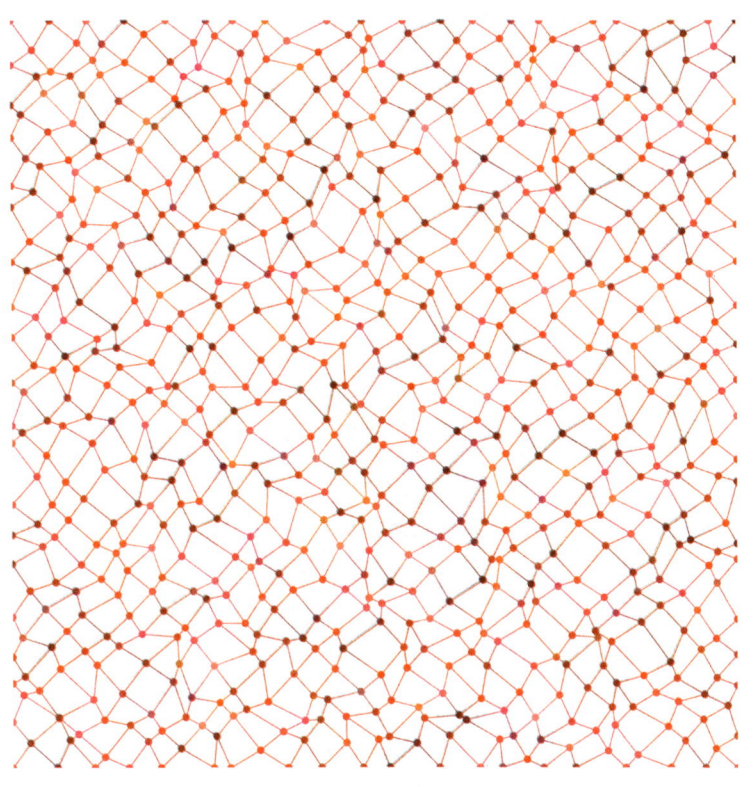

Figure 7

Heat thus released by the human body affects those parts of the universe that are nearest to it – we warm up the air/objects adjacent to us.

Electromagnetic energy emitted by the human brain is related to the emotions that humans experience; the latter are associated with changes inside the neurons, or brain cells. The wavelengths of human emotions range between 10,000 and 20,000 km approximately (see more details below in the next section). To compare, in the electromagnetic spectrum (see figure 9), the longest known wavelength belongs to radio waves and is only 100 km.

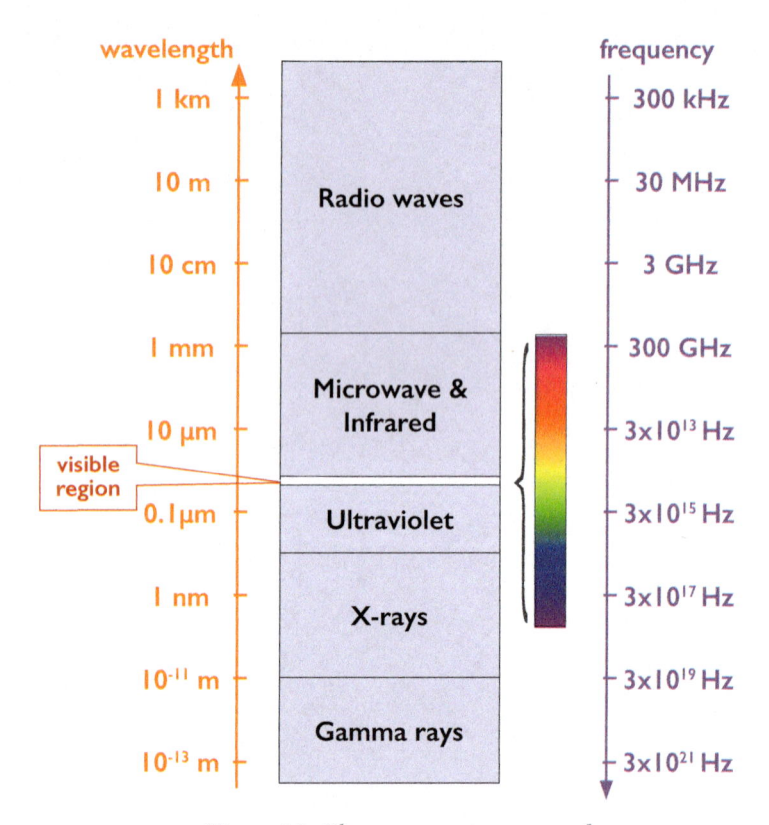

[Figure: Electromagnetic spectrum chart showing wavelength (left axis) from 1 km to 10⁻¹³ m and frequency (right axis) from 300 kHz to 3×10²¹ Hz, with regions labeled: Radio waves, Microwave & Infrared, Ultraviolet, X-rays, Gamma rays; visible region indicated between Infrared and Ultraviolet.]

Figure 10. Electromagnetic spectrum[5]

The emotion waves, or brainwaves, can be measured and recorded by a method called EEG. During EEG, electromagnetic activity of brain cells is registered on the surface of the scalp by the electrodes attached to it.

The most frequently used method to classify EEG waveforms is by their frequency – shown in brackets. The commonly studied brainwaves include delta (0.5 to 4 Hz), theta (4 to 7 Hz), alpha (8 to 12 Hz), sigma (12 to 16 Hz), beta (13 to 30 Hz) and gamma (more than 30 Hz).

---

5. "Electromagnetic radiation", NASA, https://lambda.gsfc.nasa.gov/product/suborbit/POLAR/cmb.physics.wisc.edu/tutorial/light.html [accessed 28 April 2024].

(Please note that human brainwaves are not shown on figure 9; but if they were, their place is above the radio waves.)

Delta waves are associated with deep relaxation and restorative sleep. Theta waves are common in people who are in trance or hypnotised. Alpha waves occur when awake, quiet, with eyes closed. Beta waves are the most common high-frequency waves, seen during wakefulness. Gamma waves are essential for learning, memory and processing, and combine sensory tools for processing new information.[6]

When studying emotions via EEG, high-frequency bands (beta and gamma) give a better result than low-frequency bands.[7]

OK, so we can say that brainwaves most commonly associated with emotions have a frequency of 13 Hz and above. Brainwaves are electromagnetic waves, and all electromagnetic waves travel at the speed of light (c = 299,792,458 m/s) in vacuum.

What is the wavelength of brainwaves?

Wavelength can be calculated by dividing the speed of the wave by the wave frequency, so for waves with a frequency of 13 Hz, the wavelength will be 23,060,958 metres, or 23,061 km. For brainwaves with a frequency of 30 Hz, the wavelength will be 9,993,081 metres, or 9,993 km.

When radio waves travel in atmosphere, their speed is slower than the speed of light, but not significantly so. For example, for overland transmission, the speed is about 299,250 km/s.[8] As the wavelength of brainwaves is closer to the latter of radio waves than it is to any other part of the electromagnetic

---

6. "Survey of emotion recognition methods using EEG information", Chaofei Yu and Mei Wang, *Cognitive Robotics*, vol. 2, 2022, pp.132–146
7. "Real-time EEG-based happiness detection system", Noppadon Jatupaiboon, Setha Pan-ngum and Pasin Israsena, Hindawi, https://www.hindawi.com/journals/tswj/2013/618649 [accessed 28 April 2024].
8. "The speed of radio waves and its importance in some applications", R.L. Smith-Rose, IEEE, https://ieeexplore.ieee.org/document/1701081 [accessed 28 April 2024].

spectrum, possibly the speed of brainwaves is also not significantly decreased when they travel in the atmosphere.

Dear Friend, what do you think happens to brainwaves that are recorded at the surface of your scalp? Do they keep travelling onwards, as all electromagnetic waves usually do, or do they just disappear? Do they interact with other waves they encounter on their journey? (Please note that the official science makes no comments on either of the above.)

If we dare to consider that our brainwaves don't stop, and keep moving, whilst their wavelength is on average 16,500 km (to compare, the width of the USA is 4,500 km), then what?

We basically are the longest distance "networkers" within the universe. And on the picture of the universe's energy net, it's us who can span across the large parts of it.

As the wavelength increases, the distance the wave travels also increases. This is because longer wavelengths have lower frequencies and, therefore less energy, allowing them to travel through different mediums with less resistance and maintain their amplitude over longer distances.[9]

Is it not enormously exciting to think that the brainwaves of our emotions travel very far, and very fast, transmitting the information from us/about us?

Conventional science admits that human brainwaves are hard to study. Conventional science also seems unsure whether electromagnetic waves "ever interact with each other". And yet, every classical physics textbook tells you that waves interact with each other via mechanism of interference – see figure 11.

---

9. "Why do long wavelengths travel further than short wavelengths?", Physics Forums, https://www.physicsforums.com/threads/why-do-long-wavelengths-travel-further-than-short-wavelengths.63496 [accessed 28 April 2024].

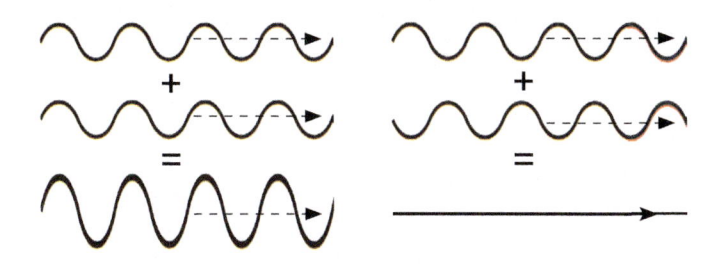

Figure 11. Constructive and destructive interference between waves

Dear Friend, despite official science being mostly silent on the matters we are discussing, luckily, there are some brave and inquisitive minds that are carrying out research into brain activity, for example, Dimitrios Pantazis, director of the Magnetoencephalography (MEG) Laboratory at MIT's McGovern Institute.[10]

As Mr Pantazis rightly says, there is no significant interference between radio waves and brainwaves, for *only waves of a similar frequency* could have significant interactions between them.

Brainwaves from different people have very similar frequencies. So if we accept that brainwaves travel on, then the brainwaves of emotions from different people encounter each other as they travel in the space outside the human bodies and interact with each other. (And yes, this would explain the phenomenon of telepathy.)

They also interact with other electromagnetic waves they encounter (emitted by other entities in the universe), the most significant interactions occurring between those waves whose frequency is identical.

When frequencies are uniform, resonance occurs, and the energy waves from the "force" (with the information they

---

10. "Can brain waves interfere with radio waves?", Elizabeth Dougherty, MIT School of Engineering, https://engineering.mit.edu/engage/ask-an-engineer/can-brain-waves-interfere-with-radio-waves [accessed 28 April 2004].

carry) are absorbed into the "entity" (as detailed in "How does the universe work: an overview" in chapter 1).

The above is the physics explanation for the transcendence, and we'll tap into medicine, too, in the next section, to make everything completely clear.

MIND, BODY AND HEART

Love is of all passions the strongest, for it attacks simultaneously the head, the heart and the senses.

– Lao Tzu

OK, so now we are ready to analyse what is happening to the man and the woman described in the previous section.

The man feels emotions of love that are generated in his brain. Those emotions give him the information on how his woman should be touched. The electromagnetic energy of his emotions (with the information it contains) travels along the nerve fibres, from emotional parts of his brain to other parts of his nervous system that are responsible for the movements of his fingers. From then on, nerve impulses travel to the nerves that end within his muscles/skin. With the information thus conveyed, he is able to touch her in exactly the right way – the way that is right for her, that is.

I love you with so much of my heart that none is left to protest.

– William Shakespeare, *Much Ado About Nothing*

It is not just his brain that is involved in the emotions of love; so is his heart. The brain releases hormones which change the way his heart beats. The nerves that connect his brain and his heart alter the way his heart muscle contracts (this could even, temporarily (did you know?), change the shape and size of the main heart chamber! Turns out, the poets have been right all along).

In turn, the heart sends messages back to the brain, reinforcing the emotions of love.

When a woman is experiencing touch that feels exactly right, the pertinent electrical and chemical signals from the receptors in her skin travel along the nervous pathways to her emotional brain. There, the emotions of love are generated. The link between her brain and her heart becomes activated, multiplying the emotions of love for her, too.

Once both a man and a woman feel emotions of love, electromagnetic waves are generated in her and his brain. A man and a woman are both simultaneously an entity and a force in relation to each other; the frequency is the same, and so the resonance occurs. Resonance implies the highest amplitude (high energy) waves. Additionally, as explained in previous sections, the frequency of romantic love is the highest amongst all a man's and woman's natural frequencies; high frequency means high energy, too. Therefore, the highest possible levels of energy that either of them are capable of are being produced.

When high-energy waves travel across their bodies, a man and a woman feel the highest possible levels of pleasure.

When the energy waves travel beyond their bodies, into space around them, they encounter other electromagnetic waves – the energy mesh of the universe. As there is a vast number of electromagnetic waves travelling in space, some of them will have the same frequency as our couple's waves, and so "resonance with the universe" also occurs.

Do you remember that during resonance, the energy of the "force" is being absorbed into the "entity"? Absorbing the waves' energy and the information within is the reason that some people describe feeling an "electric shock" (constructive interference between the waves?) or the opposite – "paralysis" (destructive interference?); or seeing light; others hearing and understanding a language they do not know; catching sight of the places they have never been to, etc.

To summarise, a couple in love generates high-energy waves that are emitted into the universe; in turn, they are absorbing energy and information from the universe that cannot be perceived by senses, becoming not only one flesh with each other but one flesh with the universe.

Dear Friend, perhaps we are now ready to answer a question we posed at the beginning of the book: "Why do we like sex so much?"

The latter, in the context of "true love" (same natural frequencies) is a reliable way to experience transcendence, or being one with the universe, which is the soul's greatest desire.

But is "sex" really the only way? How does one define it, anyway? And did you know that having loved each other for decades, a man and a woman don't just share one identical love frequency; they will have developed many of them; their resonance becomes multilevel, and then what happens is this. When he touches her hand… it takes her breath away, gives her a dizzy head, turns her legs into jelly and melts her heart all at the same time, in a fraction of a second! It used to take them half the night, when they had just met.

See this beautiful quote by Bruce Lee:

In the beginning a flame is… very pretty, often hot and fierce, but still only light and flickering. As love grows older, our hearts mature and our love becomes as coals, deep-burning and unquenchable.

ETERNAL

Love has no age, no limit; and no death.

– John Galsworthy

Dear Friend, why do you think so many modern humans are unhappy in love?

Maybe it's the fast-speed, disposable lifestyle that we are all permeated with that is to blame. We've become conditioned to expect instant gratification. Sometimes, we treat our lover as if he were a washing machine! It's much easier to get a new one than to repair an existing one, right? So once the colour blue is felt, it quickly leads to purple and that's the end of the love story for many of us; we move on... This is an illusionary improvement in our situation, though, for once the "colour red only" phase has passed with our new lover, the challenges of living through the whole rainbow do recommence. Some of us come to even more tragic ends – the poor souls who took their own lives due to the pains of love.

If they only knew that the rainbow has many colours, and one has to experience all of them... to reach the state of white love – peaceful, blissful and eternal.

Eternal... people say: "True love never dies." (Remember, "true love" is when man and woman's natural frequencies are the same.)

Writers and artists state the same a little more eloquently.

You know, the words from the song? "... *when you hold me like that... I can barely recall, but it's all coming back to me.*"

This love, so far from dying, as he hoped, was making rapid strides.

– Stendhal, Scarlet and Black

Dear Friend, can you see why this happens?

When a couple in love reaches the state of resonance (as described in the section "Mind, body and heart"), they are emitting electromagnetic waves into the space.

Those waves *(a tangible, physical essence of their love)* **become part of the energy mesh of the universe. Their "love**

energy" can be transferred to other entities, alter its form – but it cannot disappear, for energy cannot disappear. This is why, when you tune into your inner essence – your main natural frequency that is – you can bring love back. For the same reason, when your lover dies, your love does not.

JUDITH'S STORY

A woman's life is woman's loves. She was kissed a million times; he erased them all, with just one kiss.

It's been raining for days. She always loved the rain, but now was wishing for the sun – longing for it… longing to see him, too!

In the morning, when she said he could visit, the rain had suddenly stopped; the sun obediently came – his rays as warm as milk; they fondled everything they touched, then came to rest in her garden.

"Escape the shears!" – azaleas and honeysuckle are thinking secretly; huge, overgrown – they are umbrellas from the rain. Their breathing leaves are freshly washed, and, gleaming with the sun, the droplets look like crystals… and this is how he saw her – smiling face, surrounded by little diamonds, evoking trembling eyes.

The garden gate flew open… as she was passing through, he caught her and he kissed her on the lips. Deadly pale, she shook away from him…

He came back the next day; silently begging eyes, entreating her fervently…

Soon, they belonged to each other; spellbound by love, their days and nights – the never-ending dream. The summer ended; autumn came… then another one… Their forest, loved by rain, was full of mushrooms; bright autumn leaves' converted beauty – a carpet under their feet; he held her hand, sometimes for miles.

He always loved to bike. It was an accident! The driver, newly qualified, the flooded road, her hand just slipped.

She got a call. She ran like mad! Soon saw him... lying there, on his back, his eyes wide open... his poor head, must hurt so much! Covered with blood and fallen leaves – they stuck to it.

Oh no... NO! Her wail made people sick... lifted his head; his chest, so cold! The lightning thought – "He's freezing! Cover him."

Dropped down, her body guarding his, willing to warm him up, to breathe the life back in...!

Hastily kissing... his eyes, his face. Her ears deaf; thick, muddy sound in her head... The wind is muddling the strands of ivy; then flies away, oblivious to all.

When people tried, they couldn't tear her away... "... makes not a sound... freezing cold herself."

For days, she was drifting in and out of the medicated stupor; alive or dead? You really couldn't tell: her face transparent, pallid – framed by the shadow's hair; expression's want... unseeing eyes – padlocked.

One night, her mind – awoke a drop – had a hurried thought: "Pretend you are asleep!" Left alone for five minutes – she escaped.

Her father found her by the river. She almost made it to the water... collapsed – too weak; dark dress, the soaked heap of pain on moonlit grass...

Aghast, he swallowed screaming pain... Is this – my daughter? His lips made a smile, regarded her again:

Huge eyes, dead lakes of salty trickles... the messy hair everywhere – she looked a fright... He spoke to her... slowly... slowly... her gaze, unhinged and restive – it has softened; her shaking head, it paused.

"Where is he buried?"

"..."

"Ohh..." she sighed not spoke.

The winter, then the spring – they came and went. She got stronger, started to walk again in their garden; she never talked about him... no, no, she was not trying to hold on to her grief... the opposite... their little girl...! but she just couldn't... broken heart... and there was nothing anyone could do

to help with that...
but, maybe, time...?
"Grandpa, Mum doesn't really live with us anymore, does she...? Far, far away... she lives with Dad."

HOW THE UNIVERSE CONNECTS TO YOU

THE ROLE OF A HUMAN

Each one of us is an outlet to God and an inlet to God.

— Ernest Holmes

Dear Friend, the above quote makes perfect sense now, does it not? We transmit the energy and information of our brainwaves into the universe, and the energy and information of the universe (when in the resonance with our frequencies) is absorbed into us.

From chapter 1 you'll remember that a purpose of the universe is to exist whilst using its space and energy most efficiently. Are you helping the universe to achieve that goal?

Let's appraise your qualities:

1. This human is an intelligent form of life, capable of initiating and controlling the energy flow between himself and the universe.

2. The brainwaves of his emotions are able to travel farther than any other type of electromagnetic radiation.

3. When he is experiencing a long-lasting romantic love, he feels a whole range of emotions, which translates

into the greatest possible variety of frequencies of his brainwaves.

4. When he is experiencing a long-lasting romantic love, he and his lover generate high-amplitude (high-energy) brainwaves because of the resonance between the two of them. (Note that this happens whatever colour is the current phase of your love; for as long as you are both feeling blue, or both feeling red, the resonance will occur.)

5. When he is happy in love, he will experience transcendence, absorbing the waves and the information they contain from the universe.

6. His life's mission means he'll carry out the deeds that are unique to him.

Dear Friend, your qualities described above, they please the universe, very much!
A human in love is the universe's favourite entity. The universe's existence depends on the energy flow never stopping, the greatest possible variety of electromagnetic waves being generated and all entities being connected to each other. And you are starting the energy flow; producing a variety of energy waves, as well as high-energy waves, and waves that travel very far.
The universe also needs all positions to be filled, so to speak (so there are no empty spaces), and by carrying out your life's mission, you are claiming your unique position in the energy mesh of the universe, being one of the dots on the figure 7. Here it is again on the next page.

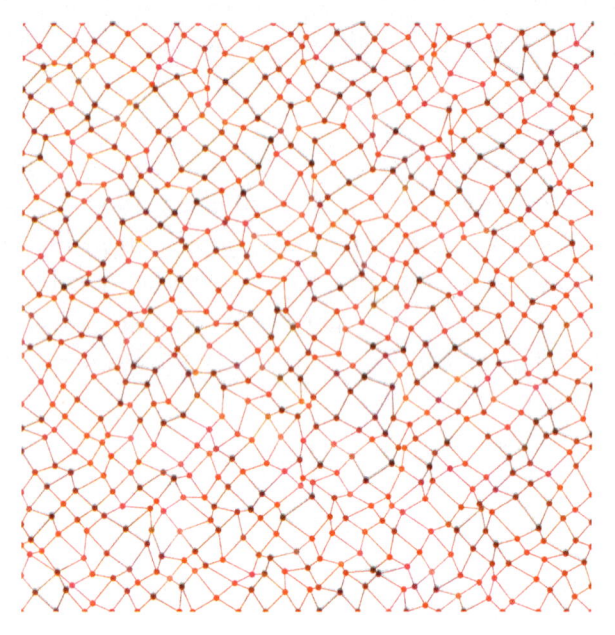

Figure 7

Does the universe care if you are happy or not? Remember we've said that the universe is cold and indifferent... and anyway, you are producing resonance-level waves whatever your emotions are – as long as you have a lover who feels the same.

However, the universe does need you to carry out your life's mission, and to produce offspring that are just as clever and capable as you. The former and the latter are far more likely to happen if you have found, and are nurturing, your very own, lasting romantic love.

HOPE, FAITH AND LOVE

No man can reveal to you nothing but that which already lies half asleep in the dawning of your knowledge.

– Khalil Gibran

Dear Friend, humanity is engaged in a centuries-long debate about the role of religion and science and their interrelationship.

Dozens of great minds have commented on the subject; see some of their opinions below.

> *Religion is regarded by the common people as true, by the wise people as false, and by the rulers as useful.*
>
> — Lucius Annaeus Seneca

> *The truths of religion are never so well understood as by those who have lost the power of reason.*
>
> — Voltaire

> *Science can purify religion from error and superstition. Religion can purify science of idolatry and false absolutes.*
>
> — Pope John Paul II

> *Science without religion is lame; religion without science is blind.*
>
> — Albert Einstein

They are all saying clever things, aren't they? But are they answering your questions?

Maybe the way to go is to simplify matters, just as Leo suggests:

> *Truth, like gold, is to be obtained not by its growth, but by washing away all that is not gold.*
>
> — Leo Tolstoy

We have already discussed that the universe is neutral and indifferent; we have devised the law of the universe accordingly — math with no frills.

We've even had the audacity to reduce the ethereal miracle of love to mere hertz and metres! Is it OK to do so? For all we are is a machine? See what Nikola says:

> *There is no conflict between the ideal of religion and the ideal of science... the universe is simply a great machine which never came into being and will never end. The human being is no exception to the natural order. Man, like the universe, is a machine.*
>
> — Nikola Tesla

Dear Friend — do you feel like you are a machine?

Perhaps the secret is to wear both hats at the same time. Romantic love is a miracle, AND love is the maths of the universe.

But the above is hard to grasp; and it's OK — because the essence of every religion is that "God is love", anyway...

> *All religions must be tolerated... for every man must get to heaven in his own way.*
>
> — Epictetus

The Bible says that the role of angels is to help people who have faith.

> *For He will order his angels to protect you wherever you go. They will hold you up with their hands...*

The Bible also says that amongst all, the angels of hope, faith and love are the most precious:

> *Hope, faith and love abide.*

When you plan to achieve something important, you are making a conscious effort to pull the energy mesh of the universe in the direction of your want.

Here, again, is figure 7 to demonstrate that.

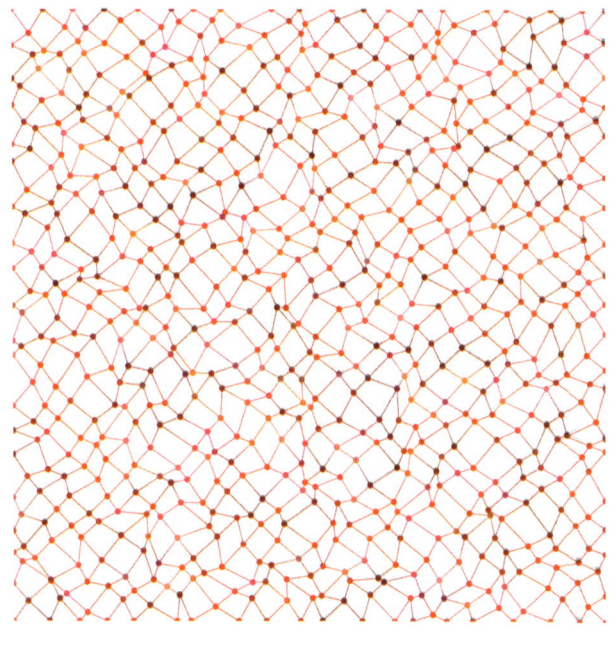

Figure 7

The direction (the red line between the dots) is "hope". "Love" is the "moving energy" that will flow along the direction that the hope shows her.

But what is "faith"? Faith is what gives the moving energy of love its speed and persistence (to avoid "stop-start-stop-start" behaviour). We are all pulling the energy blanket of the universe in different directions. Those of us who believe in our loves the most (in other words, have the greatest faith) will see their dreams come true… becoming one flesh with the universe in the process. Johann is saying the same, right?

When you are truly committed, the entire universe conspires to assist you.

– Johann Wolfgang von Goethe

Dear Friend, let us mirror the words of Johann in a metaphysical way:

When you produce your energy waves relentlessly, the maximal number of other entities with identical frequencies are enabled to respond via resonance interactions.

To summarise, in this book we have discussed – amongst other things – the physics and metaphysics; we've discovered the formula of passion, understood how romantic love enables us to both reach the highest levels of pleasure and to become one with the universe.

So this is all very good, but what do you do, dear Friend, when your sweetheart is either not at home, or too tired and fast asleep... Are there any other ways of loving the universe?

"Why is it that so many adults lie awake in their beds, between 3 and 4 a.m., and they just can't fall back to sleep?"

"It's because at that time, the veil is thin, and dark spirits are about," my friend explains. "Try talking to God, and it will make them fly away..."

I talk to God... I kiss your sleeping back... still awake.

Feeling my way up, in the darkness... carefully... I climb upstairs, and slide under the covers with our little one.

Works. Every. Time.

Cuddling my baby, I am sleeping with the angels.

Art, Interactive

The following paintings have interactive elements.

"LONE WOLF", PAGE 18

What month is his birthday? (The clue is in the sky.)

"THE TRAGEDY OF ROMANTIC LOVE", PAGE 49

Which of the following quotes do you think suits it best?

All my life, my heart has yearned for a thing I cannot name.

– Andre Breton

There is no person that love cannot heal; there is no soul that love cannot save.

– Carlos Santana

The god of love lives in a state of need. It is a need. It is an urge. It is a homeostatic imbalance. Like hunger and thirst, it's almost impossible to stamp out.

– Plato

Pains of love be sweeter far than all other pleasures are.

– John Dryden

There is scarcely any passion without struggle.

— Albert Camus

Love takes off the masks that we fear we cannot live without and know we cannot live within.

— James Baldwin

"THE RAINBOW OF LOVE", PAGE 57
One green lizard and two green snakes (representing jealousy and envy) are sneaking through the other colours. Can you see them?

"DON'T JUST UNDRESS ME, TEASE ME... SCARE ME A LITTLE...", PAGE 68
There is a man and a lady in a bikini in this painting. He is gazing at her from above. You will never look at the cherries the same away again!

"DARK LOVE", PAGE 74
Can you find all twenty-two monsters?

"WHITE HEART", PAGE 102
Did you know that lilies can hug?

Bibliography

"Broken Heart Syndrome: Evolving Molecular Mechanisms and Principles of Management", Yashendra Sethi, Hamsa Murli et al. J Clin Med, Jan 2023

"Can brain waves interfere with radio waves?", Elizabeth Dougherty, MIT School of Engineering, https://engineering.mit.edu/engage/ask-an-engineer/can-brain-waves-interfere-with-radio-waves [accessed 28 April 2004]

"Electromagnetic radiation", NASA, https://lambda.gsfc.nasa.gov/product/suborbit/POLAR/cmb.physics.wisc.edu/tutorial/light.html [accessed 28 April 2024]

Émile Zola, *Nana*, 1880

"Global Warming", http://www.livescience.com/7366-global-warming-spurearthquakes-volcanoes.html [accessed 28 April 2024]

"Gravitational Dynamics", Center for Astrophysics, Harvard & Smithsonian, https://www.cfa.harvard.edu/research/topic/gravitational-dynamics [accessed 28 April 2024]

Guy de Maupassant, *Bel-Ami*, 1885

Honoré de Balzac, *Béatrix*, 1839

Leo Tolstoy, *Anna Karenina*, 1878

"Survey of emotion recognition methods using EEG information", Chaofei Yu and Mei Wang, *Cognitive Robotics*, vol. 2, 2022, pp.132–146

"Real-time EEG-based happiness detection system",

Noppadon Jatupaiboon, Setha Pan-ngum and Pasin Israsena, Hindawi, https://www.hindawi.com/journals/tswj/2013/618649 [accessed 28 April 2024]

Stendhal, *Love*, 1822

Stendhal, *Scarlet and Black*, 1830

The Bible, New Revised Standard Version Catholic Edition, https://www.biblegateway.com [accessed 28 April 2024]

"The speed of radio waves and its importance in some applications", R.L. Smith-Rose, IEEE, https://ieeexplore.ieee.org/document/1701081 [accessed 28 April 2024]

"Why do long wavelengths travel further than short wavelengths?", Physics Forums, https://www.physicsforums.com/threads/why-do-long-wavelengths-travel-further-than-short-wavelengths.63496 [accessed 28 April 2024].

About the Author

Dr Jasmine has been a doctor for almost 30 years; she lives and works in Great Britain. She is married with two children, and her favourite pastimes include painting, playing piano, swimming and gardening.

You can find more information on her books and art here: www.makesenseofyourworld.com

Or contact her by email: info@makesenseofyourworld.com

Printed in Great Britain
by Amazon